D0903731

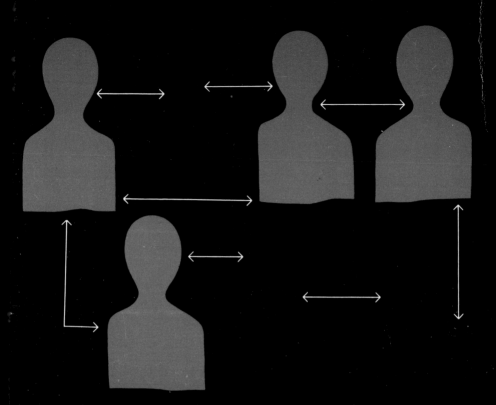

Sociology:
Concepts and Concerns

Alan F. Jensen

Sociology: Concepts and Concerns

Sociology:
Concepts and Concerns

Alan F. Jensen
Chico State College

with

Homer C. Metcalf
Chico State College

⊢ p 21

**Rand McNally
& Company
Chicago**

RAND MCNALLY SOCIOLOGY SERIES
Edgar F. Borgatta, *Advisory Editor*

Copyright © 1971 by Rand McNally & Company
All rights reserved
Printed in U.S.A. by Rand McNally & Company
Library of Congress Catalogue Card Number 75-160334

Preface

The purpose of this small text is to present in a parsimonious yet systematic fashion the basic concepts necessary for the understanding of social phenomena.

The text is not an encyclopedic inventory of all sociological observations or concepts. Nor is it a social problems text dealing with the specific problem areas of race and ethnic relations, population problems, the demise of community, demographic and ecological problems, or war and conflict. The author leaves that to the specialized texts and anthologies for coverage.

Basically, then, the text is geared to introduce sociology to newcomers to the field. It is also planned to supplement the problems courses for students who have not had introductory material. Its succinctness suggests that it can be digested with an economy of time so that the special interests of the instructor may be pursued while a major portion of a quarter or semester still remains.

Apart from its instructional value, it is hoped that the book will be a useful source for the casual reader who may want to know something of this new and burgeoning enterprise called sociology.

AFJ

Chico, California
1971

Acknowledgments

Many individuals have been instrumental in bringing this book to publication. Their contributions range from informal suggestions to elaborate critiques. Those who have given their moral support and/or technical competence throughout the project have done so most graciously and I am appreciative.

I am especially grateful to Prof. Homer Metcalf, whose ideas and fertile imagination sparked the initiation of this project and added vitality to it throughout the writing. He has been a constant source of suggestion, critique, and inspiration.

Many of my colleagues and friends have shown constant interest and have offered suggestions during the preparation of the manuscript. My special thanks to Raymond Tennyson, Prof. Richard Ogles, Prof. James Haehn, Prof. Julio Quinones, Prof. James Erickson, Prof. Lawrence Wenzel, and Prof. Robert Rankin for their help.

In the process of learning about and developing an appreciation for the field of publishing, I have received much good advice from Mr. John Freeman of Dorsey Press, Mr. Nicholas Van Male, formerly of Prentice-Hall, and from Mr. James Van Loan of Harcourt Brace Jovanovich.

My appreciation and gratitude to Mr. Lawrence Malley, Mr. Michael Kitz-Miller, Mr. Alan Newbold, and Prof. Edgar Borgatta of Rand McNally for their understanding, forbearance, and patience in their dealings with a stubborn sociologist, which is small recompense indeed for their contribution.

Mrs. Ann S. Jablin, college department editor at Rand McNally, has given competent attention to the editing and production of this manuscript, for which I am grateful.

Finally, to my wife, Sandra, for the hours of typing, editing, countless suggestions regarding content and style, and her constant moral support, I say, thank you.

Contents

How people are arranged in hierarchies of prestige and how this relates to society and the individual.

Religion as an institution of social legitimacy acts as a cohesive agent for society and provides certain buffers for the individual.

How people in secondary associations work together to achieve complex goals; how this affects the individual and how he reacts; and the consequences of bureaucratization for a greater society.

An analysis of behavior which falls outside of the working norms of a society.

A brief analysis of the agents operating to produce change in society.

A definition of social systems describing their structure and workings and the interface between systems.

Part I

Individual Action and Collective Participation

Rules

Relationships

Self

Society

Chapter 1   What Is This Thing Called Sociology?

One of the first questions raised by students in an introductory sociology class, and a question that keeps some sociologists awake at night is, "What is sociology, anyway?" It is not an easy question to answer. There are almost as many sociologies as there are sociologists, if you answer it in one way. If you answer it in another way, there is one sociology. The former answer deals with the "content" of the multitudinous essays dealing with the social world; the latter deals with the "method" of a science that is concerned with a specific piece of the experiential pie we call social phenomena.

At this point it would not be helpful to get into a diatribe on whether or not sociology is a science—some comments will be presented on this issue later in the chapter. It may be helpful, however, to talk about sociology as a way of sensitizing oneself to human society, or as a way of perceiving the world of the "social."

Now perhaps you are wondering, "What is the social world?" or "What is society?" If so, you are in good company, for this is the main preoccupation of sociologists. They will probably tell you something to the contrary as the question is always gnawing at them. A definite conclusive answer to this question isn't available—at least at this stage. However, there have been, over the years, at least three very intelligent approaches to this problem. A cursory overview of these might help you get some idea of what is meant by "society" or "the social" or "social phenomena" and how complex the conceptual problem is.

So . . . let's take a look at some general concerns of Pitirim Sorokin, Emile Durkheim, and Talcott Parsons.

Pitirim Sorokin: Sociocultural Reality   Sorokin argues for the existence of a reality (social and cultural) that is not immediately observable. That is to say, the reality of society is a reality of meanings and values, and obviously, meanings and values are not immediately observed. For greater impact, here's an example.

On my desk is a rather ornate coffee cup. It has a picture of a matador on it. It has a physical reality that is observable and can be documented. To begin with, the cup is about six inches high, is tubular, has a circumference of about six inches, is white, with the matador done in shades of brown. It has a few stains on the bottom and around the lip, a rather elegantly curved handle and is made of impervious material. But it is more than that, and this *more* is not observable immediately. This *more* is the meaning and value of the cup to me and/or to others sharing the same social organization with me. To the author, personally, that cup is the receptacle of the Scandinavian staff of life—coffee—the best of earthly drinks. That cup stands as a symbol and monument to warmth and sustenance. To a Ubangi tribesman or to a man from Mars it might be seen as an object of worship or as an object for a mystic ritual.

So it is with each object, each word, each gesture that is repeatable in our own social organization. The shared meaning is the "superorganic" in Sorokin's terms. Or more generally, it is referred to as "culture." More about that later.

Emile Durkheim: Emergent Characteristics Very generally, and in an oversimplified way, the author views Durkheim's approach as a continuation of the old philosophical game called, "How many parts make a whole?" or "Did Mrs. Murphy's chowder taste any different after the overalls were thrown in?" To wit, Durkheim felt that society was appreciably more than just an adding together of a lot of people. Or, to put it another way, society is an entity in and of itself and has characteristics which are not observable in the separate parts which make it up.

I will help you clarify that with another mundane example. Some time ago, the author opened a cardboard box, the contents of which included an odd assortment of many pieces of plastic of different shapes and sizes, two spools of thread, and some tubes of enamel. Today, there sits on his coffee table a lovely replica of the HMS *Beagle* with full rigging and colors flying. The reader will agree that the plastic parts in the box and the HMS *Beagle* are one and the same, but not really the same. We have added nothing to the original parts, but the completed model is a thing quite different from the box of assorted plastic parts. It has qualities and characteristics independent of the nature of any one or all of the parts. What is unique in the finished model is that the parts have been put into a particular relationship vis-à-vis one another according to instructions, which gives the completed model an existence of its own—a certain essence not found in the parts themselves.

So it is with Durkheim's notion about the reality of society. It is a thing in and of itself (sui generis). As a consequence of this sort of thinking about society, Durkheim was able to make a breakthrough in the analysis of suicide. He was able to relate suicide rates to certain specific peculiarities of different social organizations (societies and sub-societies).

In brief, secularized industrial societies exhibited higher rates of suicide than did the sacred agrarian societies. In industrial societies, the parts are arranged in such a way as to set the individual alone in a sea of vagueness; that is, the individual has no standard for the proper rules for behavior and he is required to depend upon his own judgment for the distribution of his fortunes. In agrarian societies, the individual is solidly included in a highly stable world of specific rules (norms) by which he can pattern his activity.

Talcott Parsons: System of Action   Parsons refers to the "social" as one of three systems of processes which together account for human actions. The three systems are: (1) the personality, (2) the society, and (3) the culture. The personality system is made up of an organization of the actor's personal needs and his dispositions toward the objects which make up the world he lives in. These objects are physical (things in the environment), social (other people and their personalities), and cultural (meanings, values, and norms).

The social system is the observable structuring of relationships between the many personalities. And, the cultural system is the organization of the rules (norms), values, and meanings which govern and give credence to the social relationships. To Parsons, human social behavior is activity directed at achieving a goal and satisfying a need (action). The behavior is understandable and predictable to a certain extent as the consequence of the interaction of these three systems. It is so only to a certain extent because these three systems and what they encompass are very vague. The following diagram may help to explain this relationship.

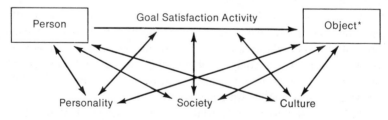

*And its value and meaning.

These ideas will be discussed in more detail later.

By now you should have some idea as to what is meant by "the social" or "social reality" or "social behavior." However, this does not answer the question, "What is sociology?" but at least we now have some shared language to work with. To begin to answer the question, the author would say at the outset that sociologists are those scholars and researchers who attempt to describe and understand the way in which the parts of society are put together, how the structure affects individual behavior, how individual behavior affects the structure, and how the structure changes over time. Granted that is too simplified and too vague an answer, but it will suffice for now. Perhaps we can get a little closer to the answer in the coverage of the next two topics. With this in mind, let's look at the origins of the discipline and at what kinds of things are being done by people called sociologists.

Science and Sociology Begging the question, the following is one position on the place of personal values in the scientific enterprise. Just about every one of the introductory texts in sociology tells its readers that the sociologist in his scientific activities cleanses his work of personal bias and seeks objectivity. Imagine, if you will, the image that accompanies the word "objectivity" in your thoughts. Is it not that of a white-coated, sharp-featured, bright-eyed, untiring researcher with clean fingernails? If not that, it's the image of some seeker of wisdom and truth of an eternal and impeccable variety. Perchance you see a bust of Plato. At any rate, your image is one of all the good and shining attributes of the unbiased practitioner of sound reason and clear thinking. I congratulate you for such a lovely image, but your slip is showing. You, my friend, are biased, as are any of us who would impose his image of objectivity on the world when deciding what is a science and what is not. But then again, we must have some criteria by which to be critical and thus maintain our skepticism.

There are many steps in the scientific enterprise, many phases in the development of a science, and many modes of objectivity representative of each of these phases. It is the experience of the author that these steps prevail:

1. Early casual observation.
2. Initial reporting.
3. More specific description.

4. Classification and delineation of the variables or parts of the phenomena being studied.
5. Development of specific hypotheses.
6. Structured, controlled experimental observation.
7. Reporting the findings.
8. Repetition of the experiments.
9. Development of general statements of law-like nature which state the relationship between the elements of the phenomena being studied.
10. Development of a theory.
11. Explanation of new observations or prediction of future states of affairs.

If this is the natural history of a scientific investigation, and if a science grows through phases, each characterized by a predominance of activity of one particular step, then the author sees sociology as being in a phase characterized by step 5 activity, having progressed with some degree of completeness through the other four. This also means that the nature of objectivity involved is consistent with our relative maturity as a science. With that in mind, let us briefly examine the historical developments which have led to sociology.

Origins of Sociology   If our concern is with thinkers and researchers who seek to know the nature of society, we could begin by going back to Moses and the Hebrew prophets or even back to the Chaldeans whose thoughts preceded those of the Hebrews. That would be an arduous task indeed, and one much better accomplished by historians and philosophers. Instead, we shall summarize briefly the intellectual developments since the eighteenth century, during which time the scientific revolution greatly altered man's thinking about his place in the universe and in society.

The period of Western history referred to as The Enlightenment saw the ever-increasing concern for putting man in the "driver's seat" of his small, but expanding, physical universe. It was revolutionary indeed that the idea that knowledge of physical and natural relationships provided the ability to predict and control these for human ends. But even more revolutionary (and upsetting to some) was the idea that what proved to be workable in regard to physical phenomena might also be applied to the world of social and human phenomena.

This idea, based on the results of yet immature physical sciences, gave rise to a more secular image of man and his society in the minds of Western intellectuals. To look at society and its workings as something beyond the efforts of human genius was no longer acceptable to an increasing number of philosophers and statesmen. When man began to explore the idea that things could be different, that alternatives existed, it was not surprising that after the scientific revolution there were more than two centuries of social and political revolution in human history, with changes occurring at a geometric rate.

In the nineteenth and twentieth centuries great strides were made toward the development of cultural anthropology and sociology. One can imagine a McLuhanist film of men who contributed to this advancement flashing across the screen: Karl Marx, Herbert Spencer, Emile Durkheim, Max Weber, George Herbert Mead, Talcott Parsons, Amitai Etzioni. All these men were, to a greater or lesser extent, dissatisfied with the continuous outpouring of untested opinions and wishful thoughts about the nature of social organization and the misconceptions which resulted. This is not to say that the work of these men was always value-free and sanitized of any preconceptions. It is simply to say that they recognized their limitations and sought to be as sound in their analyses as they could. In other words, they were skeptical, critical, and objective.

Desire for change, fear of change, disillusionment with plans and social designs that did not work made man ever more conscious of his social world and increased his demand for knowledge about it. This demand set the stage for the development of the social sciences in general and sociology in particular.

Chapter 2 Traditional Sociological Thought: The Active vs. Passive Orientation

Amitai Etzioni in his recent book, *Active Society,* brings into contemporary debate an issue that is very old and worn but won't, to all appearances, allow itself to be settled. In its earliest form the debate was between proponents of "free will" vs. "the will of God." Later it was between "free will" and "collective will." In contemporary terms the debate is between proponents of "man as an active agent" (wielder of power), as opposed to man and personality resulting from a deterministic process. This is precisely the issue that brought about the so-called "humanist" movement in the seventeenth century arts and sciences and which long before had kept St. Augustine awake nights.

The basic question then is whether man determines his own behavior, or whether man's behavior is determined by his physical and social environment. At the risk of redundance, the question could also be phrased as follows: Does man consciously control the conditions of society, or do these conditions control him? Those thinkers who believe that man is in control will be said to have an active image of man (for purposes of this text); those who are convinced that man's behavior is predetermined will be said to have a passive image of man. To explain further, an active image is one in which man comprehends his own socialization and can be an active social, political, and economic agent. A passive image, on the other hand, reflects man as a passive receptacle of culture and a passive pawn of deterministic natural law.

It should be apparent to the reader at the outset that if a sociologist has an active orientation, he will perceive the purpose of sociology and the role of the sociologist quite differently from the sociologist who has a passive conception of man.

The current debate on this issue takes on more subtleties than earlier debates, but does not solve the problem entirely. Etzioni's account is, no doubt, the most cogent, and one would assume that it is a harbinger of a generation or so of sociologists whose basic assumptions will be action oriented.

Interestingly enough, many contemporary sociologists are fairly committed to a deterministic approach. Presently, there is also a revolution that is taking place in sociological circles of the young Ph.D.s—a revolution in favor of the active image of man. It's anyone's guess why the recent shift to the active image has taken place. The author would venture the hypothesis that the intense interest of students with existentialism of the French variety has fostered this in part, along with the recognition in the nuclear age that survival is possible, and it requires doing something. In addition, there is the intellectual realization today that power is a proper phenomenon of sociological investigation.

It remains to be seen, therefore, how far-reaching this movement will become in contemporary sociological circles. It is the author's purpose in this chapter to recount in intellectual traditions the fluctuations between the active and passive assumptions in the nature of man and human society. This will not mean, however, an inventory of all great men in the history of philosophy and science; rather, the concern is with thinkers of the last century or so who have been cast in the role of sociologists. In

Chapter 3 the thoughts of contemporary sociologists will be discussed.

The thinkers to be considered may be placed in the following approximate time spans:

Late eighteenth and early nineteenth centuries

Auguste Comte (1798–1857)
Herbert Spencer (1820–1903)
Karl Marx (1818–1883)

Late nineteenth and early twentieth centuries

Emile Durkheim (1858–1917)
Georg Simmel (1858–1918)
Max Weber (1864–1920)
George Herbert Mead (1863–1931)
Robert Michels (1876–1936)

Mid-twentieth century

E. A. Ross (1866–1951)
José Ortega y Gasset (1883–1955)

Auguste Comte   Comte is often called the "father of sociology" because his "positivistic philosophy" was a reaction to the idealistic and intuitive approach of traditional philosophy. Positivism means the tendency to restrict explanations of phenomena to the phenomena themselves—in short, explanation by observation.

In its pure sense, positivism should be diametrically opposed to organicism, which views the world as a whole made up of interrelated parts. In this view, the world is thought to be analogous to the body as an organism. In Comte's writings, however, these two world views are combined.

Irving Zeitlin indicates that Comte's theories have been described as "little more than scientific rationale for a totalitarian society."[1] This is understandable because Comte lived in the post-revolutionary era in France, and he was concerned with

---

[1] Irving Zeitlin, *Ideology and the Development of Sociological Theory* (Englewood Cliffs, N. J.: Prentice-Hall, 1968), p. 57.

providing a conservative alternative to the excesses of the French Revolution.

Comte conceived of society as an organic whole characterized by developmental stages. True to his conservative position, he maintained that the philosophy of revolution had made its contribution to progress and had been surpassed, just as the theological and the metaphysical periods had.

Comte's basic tenet was that ideas govern the world or throw it into chaos. Hence, one could say that Comte had an active orientation: that man could change the course of history by changing his ideas. Lessons could be learned from past historical-ideological periods which could contribute to the improvement of man's condition in each succeeding stage. It should be remembered, however, that while Comte contemplated social change, he hoped to change society to an authoritarian social order, not to a socialistic utopia.

Herbert Spencer   While Comte technically rejected the idea of the organic model (although he utilized it implicitly to some degree), Spencer's sociology was, from start to finish, explained on the basis of an organic model. In fact, Spencer's writings greatly influenced Darwin. The book, *Social Statics,* Spencer's first publication, preceded the appearance of Darwin's *Origin of the Species* by nine years.

Herbert Spencer believed that societies, like organisms, evolved from minute units, such as primitive wandering tribes, into large masses, or societies. The increase in the social mass (society) resulted from an increase in its structure, which we now call differentiation, or increasing division of labor. As differentiation increased, the parts of the mass (individuals) became greatly interdependent, so much so, in fact, that separation became fatal to the individual parts.

Knowing this about Spencer's philosophy, one can easily understand his statement that "the citizen's life is made possible only by due performance of his function in the place he fills, and he cannot wholly free himself from the beliefs and sentiments generated by the vital connexions hence arising between himself and society."[2] In other words, because of the extreme inter-dependence of parts in a highly developed state of societal evolution, an individual is inextricably tied to the society of which he is a member. Therefore, one would conclude that Spencer's theory represents a fairly deterministic sociology of knowledge and action; that he was a passive theorist, according to our definition.

Karl Marx   Karl Marx lived at the outset of the industrial revolution, when the theory of laissez-faire capitalism was operating in practice. Marx was deeply disturbed by the conditions of the workers, and his ideas were greatly influenced by their plight.

Marx believed that society is essentially polarized into two classes, which he called the bourgeoisie and the proletariat. The proletariat he saw as being exploited by the property-owning industrialists. People who found themselves in the middle class (bourgeoisie), according to Marx, would be forced into one group or the other because they would either be able to compete with the industrialists, or, if unable to do so, would lose their businesses and fall into the working class. As more bourgeoisie moved into the working class, it increased the revolutionary potential as ex-members of the middle class would have an enlightening influence.

Marx saw the conflict between the bourgeoisie and the proletariat as a dialectical process, an idea which he gained largely from Hegel, a philosopher of the late eighteenth century. Very briefly, Hegel believed that the mind is the core of reality; hence, change reflects changes in ideas. Hegel was convinced that thought is a process. As a process, any particular idea cast up by thought (thesis) necessarily results in the evoking of its opposite (antithesis). Therefore, thought must reconcile the conflict (synthesis). This process is dialectical, which means that change results from a clash of opposites. Basically, Marx agreed with the central dialectical theme of Hegel, but where Hegel was concerned with a metaphysical reality, Marx applied the dialectic to the realm of economics. For example, feudalism collapsed be-

---

[2] Herbert Spencer, *The Study of Sociology* (New York: D. Appleton & Co., 1873), p. 73.

cause of the rise of the middle class; hence, Marx believed that capitalism would also be overthrown because of the rise of the proletariat. In his short book, *The Communist Manifesto* (which was written with his close friend and collaborator, Friedrich Engels), Marx urged members of the proletariat to "rise up, and throw off your capitalist yoke."

Marx and Engels believed that the history of all human society is the history of class struggles. Political struggles are in effect class struggles because the administrative structure of the state is nothing more than a committee managing the affairs of the bourgeoisie.

Marx's ideas present a mixture of the notions of active and passive. On the one hand, man's condition is determined by the economic structure of his environment (passive); on the other hand, man may change his environment by changing his economic structure (active). Marx saw his own role as one of enlightening the proletariat regarding the need to change the economic structure in order to end its exploitation by the industrial elites.

Emile Durkheim   While Comte is often referred to as the "father of sociology" because he invented the word, sociology, Emile Durkheim could legitimately be considered the true forerunner of today's sociologist, as he utilized a "scientific" method in the study of human behavior. He believed that behavior was explainable within a framework which was different from the more traditional approaches of psychology or biology—namely, by examining a separate entity, society itself. Durkheim taught the first course in sociology in France in Bordeaux in 1887 and became the first professor of sociology at the university in 1896. In 1902, he was appointed to the Sorbonne as a professor of education; his title was changed in 1913 to professor of "the science of education and sociology."

Durkheim had a command of the classical languages— Hebrew, Greek, and Latin, in addition to German, French, and English. He was also acquainted with philosophy, psychology, biology, anthropology, economics, political science, law, religion, literature, art, and education. For this reason, he was sometimes referred to by his students as "a modern Aristotle." He was a prolific writer and most of his works are still studied by sociologists today, particularly *The Rules of the Sociological Method, The Division of Labor in Society,* and *Suicide.*

In *Suicide,* a monumental work, Durkheim attempted to show the relationship of individual acts to the social structure by studying *rates* of suicide, not by analyzing individual acts of suicide. In order to do this, Durkheim selected a number of factors potentially related to suicide (today call them variables): religious affiliation, marriage and family, and political and national communities. It is this technique of attempting to determine particular categories related to phenomena in society by counting the number (or rate) occurring in each category which is primarily practiced by sociologists today.

One of the most elusive yet important concepts resulting from *Suicide* was what Durkheim called anomic suicide, or the condition of *anomie.* To understand anomic suicide, one must first accept Durkheim's premise that the individual's needs and the satisfaction of those needs are regulated by society, or institutions within that society, as the church or the family. In addition, the individual learns certain beliefs and practices from society or its substructures; hence, the individual is a manifestation of what Durkheim referred to as the "collective conscience."

Anomie enters the picture when a harmonious relationship no longer exists between an individual's needs (and their satisfaction) and his beliefs and practices. For example, Durkheim found that suicide rates were higher among divorced than married persons. (One must keep in mind that divorce has become partially acceptable in this society only in the last ten to fifteen years.) Therefore, one could see how, in a predominantly Catholic country in the early twentieth century, if an individual sought to meet his personal needs by terminating a marriage, this would most certainly bring his behavior into conflict with his learned beliefs and the practices of society at large. Therefore, this person would find himself disoriented, or suffering from anomie.

Durkheim also found that suicide rates were higher among Protestants than Catholics, from which he concluded that the wider the freedom one had to choose in what he believed in in Protestantism, the wider realm of uncertainty his behavior had in meeting proper standards. On the other hand, the behavioral dictates of Catholicism are well codified and fairly rigid so that an individual feels quite secure in regard to his behavior and its relationship to acceptable practices.

Hence, one could conclude from even this cursory description of *Suicide* that Durkheim had a passive image of man, that is, his studies indicated to him that man's behavior is largely determined by a complex interrelationship of economic, social, and cultural factors.

Georg Simmel   In his book, *Conflict,* Simmel develops a general model concerned with the positive effects of inter- and intragroup conflict. He uses the term "function" in this regard, but not in the organic sense as it is used by Spencer or Durkheim.[3] Functions are those consequences which result in an increase in the adaptation or adjustments of particular social relationships within an established structure. Simmel maintained that necessary ingroup and outgroup distinctions are established in and through conflict in which the outgroup may be emulated as well as resented. He indicated that there is "realistic" conflict, the motive of which is to obtain some specific goal, and there is also "unrealistic" conflict, the goal being conflict itself. The absence of conflict within a relationship cannot serve as an index of its underlying stability; rather, if incumbents feel that the system is stable, and they are secure in that fact, they will not repress feelings of hostility, but express them. Likewise, conflict with outside influences on the group will increase the cohesion of the group. Conflict with another group defines group structure and its parameters: it also helps to control ingroup conflicts before they increase to the degree that might destroy the group. Certain newly developed groups may seek to attract enemies to maintain cohesion by provoking animosity with an outside group. Then, when the

---

[3] Georg Simmel, *Conflict,* trans. Kurt H. Wolff (Glencoe, Ill.: The Free Press, 1955).

system ages and becomes rigid and bureaucratic, or if it suffers defeat or increased out-group pressure, it may turn upon itself.

In addition, conflict may establish and maintain a balance of power between political and economic interest groups within a society. At any time that a society becomes unbalanced in favor of one value system and begins to grow rigid, associations and coalitions develop, strife results; then with the accomplishment of a settlement or a conciliation there is a new balancing of forces, a new assessment of relative power. The writer would classify Simmel as one who utilizes an active orientation with an optimistic view of history. The idea implicit in his work is that development of conflict results from active volition and that a balance of power requires active participation.

Max Weber[4]   It should be observable to the reader that first assumptions not only affect one's conceptualizations about social relations, but also profoundly affect one's methodology. To Weber, the aspect which separates natural science from "spiritual" science (sociology, anthropology, history) or the science of "valuation" (meaning) is "Verstehen" (understanding). This gives the social scientist an advantage: "We can understand the actions and the subjective intentions of the actors." In short, we can grasp the meaning because we can in some way transfer to this situation the intentions that we were aware of during some past action of our own. These assumptions lead one logically to assume that Weber's orientation is an active orientation. The individual is aware of his motives and understands the motives of others and of collectives. The author concludes that Weber's orientation is one of an active, rational nature of man and, therefore, is a more optimistic view. Mankind's development is hopefully oriented toward rational structures which man actively designs and brings into existence. Weber is in some ways a modern Luther who tells us that we can work out our own societal salvation.

---

[4] This characterization is taken from N. S. Timasheff, *Sociological Theory: Its Nature and Growth* (New York: Random, 1967), pp. 175–186.

George Herbert Mead[5]   Mead was the most polished of the pragmatic triumvirate (James-Dewey-Mead) insofar as the author can determine. He devised the most understandable synthesis of pragmatic philosophy—sociology and psychology. Expanded knowledge was the tool that the sociologist could use for attaining the goal of enriched life for all men. He reiterated time and time again, "It is not to find out how we can get from a state of mind to an object outside the mind, but how intelligence that is within nature can so reorganize its experience that the activities of the inhibited individual can proceed. . . . Logic grows out of something for the sake of something."

His form of pragmatic-active behaviorism depended heavily on linguistics (signs, symbols, semantics). "The mind is not a substance, it is not located in the brain, rather it is the functioning of significant symbols." Thus the ultimate unit of existence, the focus of sociological investigation is the "self-caused, self-sustaining, ongoing behavior of the organism, initiated by a want or a problem and directed to the end of satisfying the want or solving the problem by means of available elements in the environment." Mind, to Mead, the active unity of consciousness, is teleological and willful. "It attends to this or that within a 'theatre of simultaneous possibilities' and thus 'carves out its world' from the stream of experience." What this all boils down to is that *doing* is more fundamental than *knowing* or *being,* or the corollary, knowing and being begin in action.

Robert Michels[6]   Michels's orientation is an active orientation as indicated by his first assumption about sociopolitical processes: "Democracy is inconceivable without organization. . . . Organization, based as it is upon the principle of least effort, that is to say, upon the greatest possible economy of effort, is the weapon of the weak in their struggle with the powerful. . . . The chances of success in any struggle will depend upon the degree to which

---

[5] P. E. Pfuetze, *Self, Society and Existence* (New York: Harper and Row, 1961), pp. 37–45.

[6] Robert Michels, *Political Parties* (Glencoe, Ill.: The Free Press, 1949).

this struggle is carried out upon a basis of solidarity between individuals whose interests are identical . . . the isolated member of the working classes is defenseless in the hands of those who are economically stronger."

Does this sound strangely contemporary? It was first written in 1915. Michels recognizes certain determinants at work but implies that such sociocultural determinants work on the individual or collective will only if you allow them to do so. He indicates that there are certain contextual situations that must be controlled by means of organization, such as size of groups, channeling of effort—a proposal very similar to Weber's. This is understandable in that the two shared a common cultural and academic heritage, if not similar class privileges. Both were Germans, Weber was from an elite family, Michels from the middle class. Weber's father was a member of the Reichstag, Michels's was active in the founding of the social democratic party. Michels's orientation is that of historical optimism, i.e., man is collectively in control of political and economic destinies—if he wills to be.

José Ortega y Gasset[7]   "There are no longer protagonists; there is only the chorus." With Ortega y Gasset we see a different kind of active orientation. Where Marx called for expression of collective will, and Michels and Durkheim prayed for solidarity of interest groups, Ortega y Gasset hoped for the maintenance of the man, the one, the individual who demanded more of himself to prevail over the masses who were by acclamation and sheer force of numbers predicted to ruin Europe by the virtue of no virtue. He wanted the substantive to prevail over the trivial. Where Marx was basically optimistic about the masses and what their rise to power would accomplish, Ortega y Gasset was very pessimistic. He could not foresee a time when the masses would be the shining example of moral-intellectual worth. He stated, "It is rare to find among working men, who might be taken as the best example of what we are calling 'the mass,' nobly disciplined minds." Also,

[7] William Taber, ed., *Man in Contemporary Society* (New York: Columbia University Press, 1962), pp. 486–506.

"Today we are witnessing the triumphs of hyperdemocracy in which the mass acts directly, outside the law, imposing its mass [sic] beliefs that it has the right to impose and to give force of law to notions born in the café."

Not only did Ortega y Gasset predict mass politics but also mass culture—the decline of substantive intellectual development. And did his predictions come true? Is the group, as Kierkegaard said, the great untruth? We have already seen the rise of Hitler and the Nazi Party and American television. On the other hand, there have been unprecedented advances in technology and material well-being due to mass education in an electronic age. We also have something that neither Marx nor Ortega y Gasset dreamed could happen—property-owning masses and masses with leisure time. At any rate, one would classify Ortega y Gasset as an activist and nondeterminist, but an elitist.

E. A. Ross

> Society is, of course, a kind of fiction. There is nothing to it, after all, but people affecting one another in various ways. The thesis of this book is that from the interactions of individuals and generations there emerges a kind of collective mind evincing itself in living ideas, conventions, dogmas, institutions, and religious sentiments which are more or less happily adapted to the task of safeguarding the collective welfare from the ravages of egoism.[8]

Ross appears to be less concerned with active power relationships and more theoretically oriented toward behavioral-deterministic assumptions. He did make a distinction, however, between "natural societies" where order is worked out (natural order) not by design or art but by natural processes of a behavioral nation, and class-based societies where power relationships interfere with this natural process. He called this "class control," whereby order developed through the exercise of power by a parasitic class through and for its own interests; class con-

[8] E. A. Ross, *Social Control* (New York: Macmillan, 1928), p. 293.

trol was unnatural and led to negative consequences. Natural processes in a parsimonious, simple society were Ross's ideal. His social-psychological constructs revolved around the concepts of suggestion-imitation. The distribution of attitudes, ideas, and habits was of greater concern to him than was the concept of personality, and he was of the strong conviction that the future of sociology was in the development of statistical methods.

SUMMARY

In this chapter the author has attempted to show contemporary students, who would like to see a sociology based on first assumptions of an active orientation (such as the one presented by Etzioni), that they are not dealing with a new dialogue. The dialogue, of course, will not be settled by this generation of sociologists. We have just emerged from a decade or so of extreme determinism in which the approach of Mead was almost taboo. We are now beginning what will be at least a decade of active-oriented sociology.

Chapter 3   Images of Man
in Contemporary
Sociological Analysis

We have just gone through an account of ideas in the traditions of the discipline concerning the two general images of man's nature—the behavioral-deterministic image and the rational-action image. As was indicated, the debate between these two ways of thinking still prevails even though contemporary proponents are more sophisticated and subtle in their handling of the issues. At times they collaborate in attempting a synthesis of method and theory of the two orientations. What follows is not an exhaustive review of contemporary sociological thought, but simply an attempt to show the broad outlines of the field of sociology.

Behavioral approaches toward a microsociology:

Tamotsu Shibutani
Robert Bales
Paul Lazarsfeld

Action approaches toward a macrosociology:

Talcott Parsons
James Coleman
Amitai Etzioni

BEHAVIORAL APPROACHES TOWARD A MICROSOCIOLOGY

Tamotsu Shibutani The central concern of those who are referred to as microsociologists or social-psychologists is the concept of "motivation," i.e., what makes the human organism behave in a particular way. The focus among thinkers of this behaviorist persuasion is on the nonconscious, determined, and passive aspects of motivation. The question then becomes: What are the factors which act upon the individual to make him behave in a certain way? This is different from the action orientation which asks: What was the individual's reason in choosing this particular path of action? Shibutani in his book, *Society and Personality,* offers one of the most well-ordered syntheses of behavioral microsociology.[1]

These nonconscious and/or nonverbalized reasons for behavior seem to fall into the following four categories:

1. Preservation of a self-image.
2. Status maintenance (including not only position but self-esteem).
3. Reference group behavior.
4. The human equation.

First, let us look at the preservation of the self-image as a basis for action. Self-conceptions, self-images, or whatever you wish to call them, are regularized manners in which people act with reference to themselves. As Shibutani puts it, "A self-conception may be regarded as a stable relationship between a man as an active agent and what he consistently experiences as himself (an object of the agent)." Such behavior may be regarded as the "effort of a person to maintain his unity and integrity."

[1] Tamotsu Shibutani, *Society and Personality* (Englewood Cliffs, N. J.: Prentice-Hall, 1961), pp. 179–280.

An individual must give some sort of meaning to himself as an object; he must be able to react symbolically toward this object in his thought; he must give dimension to his object and relate this object to the whole world of objects that he deals with daily. Implicit in the self-image concept is the idea of consistency and, in this sense, it is quite akin to the concept of role behavior, i.e., observable behavior on the part of the individual in a persistent pattern allowing for predictability of behavior in selected circumstances. This, of course, changes the focus from the self to others, who, in the case of role analyses, expect or anticipate a certain consistency from the individual. These perceived expectations of others do have their cumulative effect on the development of the self-image and in this sense the two concepts are related. We assume, then, that the individual has at least two forces working upon him for the maintenance of self: first, a need for consistency as he relates his objective self to the environment; and second, certain pressures applied by others in the environment in order to maintain a behavior pattern in line with their expectations.

In addition to considering the preservation of the self-image as a basis for action, let us consider status maintenance as an element in human motivation. When selecting a mate, employing a worker, or dealing with neighbors, group members employ standards in the comparisons that ensue. These standards involve various types of criteria; for instance, one may be an evaluation of how well the individual in focus functions in helping the group attain its goals. In short, it is the behavior of the individual who is evaluated, i.e., his role behavior. We might say that this evaluation is one of attaching a value to the position in which this behavior is played; hence, this valued or ranked position becomes a status. Individuals in these ranked positions enjoy gratificational-type behavior from others if they play the role correctly, i.e., esteem and prestige.

As these valued positions are generally in short supply, the individual will compete for them in order to partake of the rewards involved and, having attained a status position, he will behave in a manner consistent with the expectations directed toward that position in order to maintain himself in that position. This also implies that the individual has some sort of aspiration level or a relative amount of desire to occupy certain positions. These also come out of the group phenomenon; namely, reference group behavior.

The third category listed is reference group behavior. Shibutani says:

> Each person acts on the basis of his definition of the situation. He categorizes the transaction in which he is involved, locates himself in it, and thereby decides upon his obligations. The consistency with which he defines a succession of situations arises from the fact that he generally uses the same perspective, one that he shares with his associates. Once he adopts a particular point of view, it becomes his working conception of the world, and he brings his frame of reference to bear upon each situation he encounters, whether or not anyone else from the group is actually on the scene. . . . The concept of reference group may be used to designate that group, real or imaginary, whose standpoint is being used as the frame of reference by the actor.[2]

Behavior, then, we assume, is predictable if, and only when, we have some understanding of the way in which the group from which the actor comes views the situation.

The fourth category of behavior determinants is bound up in the vague concept of individual and selective perception of the world. This can elicit an idiosyncratic view of, and response to, the world of objects and events. Human action then becomes less predictable unless we are familiar with the individual in question and have some indication of how he views the world, or how he senses the varied stimuli which bombard him. This uniquely individual element is referred to by Shibutani as the "human equation." One of the most dramatic examples in which the individual can show his uniqueness would be his choice of action in a critical situation, a situation in which an applicable behavior

[2] *Ibid.*, p. 250.

pattern has not as yet been prescribed. This is not the only type of situation to be sure, but in normal situations personal behavior that has unique aspects is not often noticeable. If an individual's behavior is continually at or near one extreme of the acceptable range of possible behaviors when faced with a dilemma, he may behave in a way that is completely unexpected; or if he finds himself in a situation that has no previous definition or behavior prescription, he will have to play it by ear, so to speak. Such a situation would be a crisis of some sort, a dissolution of his normal interactive system, as a natural calamity, a death, or the absence of common associates.

Robert Bales   Most of the people we have been talking about up to this point have provided fairly reasonable hypotheses regarding human action or behavior. Bales stands out as somewhat unique in that he (representative of many contemporary sociologists) marks a "take-off" point for the discipline. That is to say, the main concern of Bales is accurate description of what takes place when individuals in a group setting interact with each other in the solving of a group task. His concern is not so much with personality as it is with certain repetitive "acts" of specific individuals, or certain specific "acts" which occur over time in a group structure. Likewise, his concern is not so much with motivation as it is with how certain individuals "act" in such a way as to obtain desired "reactions" from others. Although individuals in interaction are possibly unconscious of the various act-reaction occurrences, Bales has established an observational device whereby he has observed certain recurrent patterns and processes in human interaction.[3] This highly useful device includes the classification of verbal and nonverbal acts into four basic categories of communicative acts, each having three subcategories. See Table 1.

With the aid of certain other research "hardware" and a small group observation room or laboratory, it is possible to describe quite accurately the repetitive act patterns of individuals and the

[3] Robert F. Bales, *Interaction Process Analysis* (Cambridge, Mass.: Addison-Wesley, 1950). See also, Robert F. Bales, "Small Group Theory and Research" in *Sociology Today*, Robert K. Merton, Leonard Broom, and Leonard S. Cottrell, Jr. (New York: Basic Books, 1959).

TABLE 1 Interaction Process Analysis, Categories of Communicative Acts*

Major Categories	Subcategories	Illustrative Statements or Behavior
A. POSITIVE REACTIONS	a. Shows solidarity	Jokes, gives help, rewards others, is friendly
	b. Shows tension release	Laughs, shows satisfaction, is relieved
	c. Shows agreement	Passively accepts, understands, concurs, complies
B. ANSWERS	d. Gives suggestion	Directs, suggests, implies autonomy for others
	e. Gives opinion	Evaluates, analyzes, expresses feeling or wish
	f. Gives information	Orients, repeats, clarifies, confirms
C. QUESTIONS	g. Asks for information	Requests orientation, repetition, confirmation
	h. Asks for opinion	Requests evaluation, analysis, expression of feeling or wish
	i. Asks for suggestion	Requests direction, possible ways of action
D. NEGATIVE REACTIONS	j. Shows disagreement	Passively rejects, resorts to formality, withholds help
	k. Shows tension	Asks for help, withdraws, daydreams
	l. Shows antagonism	Deflates other's status, defends or asserts self, is hostile

* Based on Robert F. Bales, *Interaction Process Analysis* and on A. Paul Hare, *Handbook of Small Group Research*, p. 66, as found in Clovis Shepherd, *Small Groups: Some Sociological Perspectives* (San Francisco: Chandler Press, 1964), p. 30.

process by which groups of individuals arrive at, or do not arrive at, consensus, and solve, or do not solve, tasks.

Paul Lazarsfeld   Paul Lazarsfeld provides a reconstruction of his analytical mode in the *Language of Social Research.* He indicated the existence of an analytical mode wherein, "The crux of the intellectual task lies not in finding regularities, but in applying available knowledge to the understanding of a particular case— be it a person or a collective." By way of example, he indicated:

> The clinical psychologist deals with one person at a time and traces, let us say, his emotional difficulties back to his childhood experiences. The historian links the events of the French Revolution back to the social factors which characterized the old regime. The anthropologist links a tribe's ideas about magic to the ways it makes its living in a specific environmental setting.[4]

He identified such studies as being under the rubric of the "empirical analysis of action." He stated:

> The purpose of such a study may be formulated in a variety of ways. Social reformers want to keep people from committing crimes; advertisers want to know how people can be made to buy their products; occupational counsellors study how people choose their jobs, because they want to turn one man's experience into another man's guidance. Whatever the purpose, all these studies have one central topic in common: What are the factors which account for the choices which people make among a specified number of alternatives.[5]

The crucial identifying characteristic of this analytical method is that causal inferences are made for each event separately at an

---

[4] Paul F. Lazarsfeld, and Morris Rosenberg, eds., *The Language of Social Research* (Glencoe, Ill.: The Free Press, 1955), pp. 387–388.

[5] *Ibid.,* p. 388. Adapted with permission of The Macmillan Company; © by The Free Press, a Corporation, 1955.

early stage in the investigation with statistical combination and summary undertaken at a later time. Lazarsfeld noted that the methodology has not been formalized, but he provides us with a reconstruction and follows this by the inclusion of some examples. A further elaboration of Lazarsfeld's reconstruction as paraphrased here includes five aspects.

First, typological distinctions are made where the researcher categorizes conditions, situations, and individuals so as to treat "cases which are fairly comparable within the frame of one's study." Second, it becomes necessary to decide on the set of factors that is to be taken into account when interpreting the observed activity. Lazarsfeld calls this set of elements an "accounting scheme." Not only are the elements listed, but here also, some typological considerations must be made in order to assess the causal role of these factors.

Third, a decision has to be made as to the best interviewing method needed to obtain the necessary data in light of the accounting scheme and other typological considerations. In this third step, Lazarsfeld indicates another demand. This is the demand of eliciting what he calls, "surplus information." He indicates that we do not want to rely exclusively on the actor's own assessment of what determined his choice. It is necessary to introduce specifying and check questions, so that in the end the investigator can make his own assessment of each single case.

Fourth, the researcher has to make a causal assessment or an interpretation linking the accounting scheme factors to the observations for each specific case, an activity which Lazarsfeld agrees is quite complicated and far from clear as to the proper procedure.

Fifth, he indicates that all cases must be combined into a statistical result with a table of "reasons" for each element in the accounting scheme. He warns that such statistical results are of a peculiar nature, supposedly because of the range of alternate interpretations possible. Based on Lazarsfeld's reconstruction, some paradigm cases of research of this kind are given to further elucidate the elements of the procedure.

Relative to the construction of accounting schemes, one

paradigm case is quite explicit in its simplicity as to what is involved in this activity. This is an article by J. Stannard Baker entitled, "A Framework for the Assessment of Causes of Automobile Accidents."[6] Baker begins by listing the conditions which in his view are necessary to make a traffic accident; this is essentially an operational definition of a traffic accident. He went on to talk about analyzing the key event—an auto accident—by noting this as the consequence of a series of events. He elaborated on the three types of causes in terms of temporal priority: (1) the early remote causes, (2) the mediate or middle causes, and (3) the direct or immediate cause. All of these factors are hypothesized as being related in a causal series he calls the "story of an accident" which constitutes a narrative of the chain of events leading to the key or consequent event. One should note, however, that such a narrative is much more explicit and self-consciously systematic than the account of a historical narrative given above.

Certain of these factors are more important than others and Baker referred to these as "landmarks in the chain of events." These are factors which are said to give a meaningful interpretation to the question, "Why this accident?" On the basis of any single accident, the accounting scheme can be brought to bear in what he calls a "reconstruction of the accident."

> We mean the process of trying to figure out afterward what happened. From information we can get following an accident, we can think back to what must have happened to produce such results. The bits of information can be fitted together to make a logical and sensible explanation of the chain of events including the direct cause and many of the mediate causes. This is like fitting together a jigsaw puzzle. Parts of the puzzle are nearly always missing, and we can only infer what the missing part of the picture is like.[7]

[6] J. Stannard Baker, "A Framework for the Assessment of Causes of Automobile Accidents," in *The Language of Social Research,* eds. Paul F. Lazarsfeld, and Morris Rosenberg (Glencoe, Ill.: The Free Press, 1955), pp. 438–448.

[7] *Ibid.,* p. 447.

ACTION APPROACHES TOWARD A MACROSOCIOLOGY

Talcott Parsons   It should be said first that the action vs. behavior categories are not mutually exclusive. For instance, Parsons has collaborated with the more behaviorally oriented theorists, as Robert Bales, in an attempt at developing a general theory. However, in broad outline Parsons' concern is with the active image of man. Furthermore, it is quite obvious that the notions and concepts used in the two orientations are exchanged to some degree. What seems to be the case is that the different approaches have different applications depending on what level of the social you are working on. The levels range from the small group (microsociology) to the total society (macrosociology). Generally speaking, the more reduced the level (microscopic), the greater is the tendency to use the behavioral approach. Parsons has attempted to develop concepts which are applicable at both levels, but his first contributions, and his continuing contributions, appear to be most applicable on the level of total society, and when he collaborates with behaviorists on the more reduced level of individual action he carries the total society way of thinking with him. We have already talked about Parsons in regard to the idea of society as a system. At this point the author would like to sketch the "action" framework which Parsons set down in collaboration with Edward Shils.[8]

> The theory of action is a conceptual scheme for the analysis of behavior of living organisms. It conceives of behavior as oriented to the attainment of ends in situations, by means of the normatively regulated expenditures of energy. There are four points to be noted in this conceptualization of behavior: (1) Behavior is oriented to the attainment of ends or goals or other anticipated states of affairs. (2) It takes place in situations. (3) It is normatively regulated. (4) It involves expenditure of energy or effort or 'motivation.'[9]

[8] Talcott Parsons, and Edward Shils, *Toward a General Theory of Action* (New York: Harper, Torchbooks, 1965), pp. 52–111.

[9] *Ibid.,* p. 53.

Moving from this quite explicit definition, Parsons and Shils go on to establish the first assumptions, the language, and the typologies in this approach. As such, this fairly recent account is an extension of Parsons's "functionalism" as it was set down in *The Structure of Social Action,* the first edition of which was published in 1937.[10]

Without becoming too involved in the terminology and the rather elaborate arguments of the Parsons and Shils paper, what are the essential ingredients of the action approach established here? The author will attempt to summarize these as succinctly as possible.

To begin with, many kinds of things converge in the situation in which action takes place. Initially, though, the concern is with the actor upon whom the analysis is focused. It is not very meaningful just to say that his action is determined by the situation in which he finds himself; important to the analysis are the things the actor brings with him into the situation. These are accounted for initially in the way he perceives things in his environment (sees the world) and the objects in his world that he likes, dislikes, or about which he couldn't care less. Certain of these objects (people and things) will be perceived as things he wants, things he doesn't want, things he wants but knows he shouldn't have, and things he doesn't necessarily want but thinks he should have anyway. These wants, of course, are built into him largely through the process by which his personality system is developed (socialization) and primarily reflect the cultural system around him. The same may be said of the shoulds and should nots. Likewise, some wants are more wanted than others, and one will expend more energy toward achieving these. Such wants are goals in the action situation and the energy one is willing to expend in their acquisition is known as motivation.

Therefore, in a particular situation, the individual will select objects as goals, the achievement of which is satisfactory to him. He chooses from alternative goals and alternative ways to achieve his goal. However, much determinism creeps into the analysis in the sense that the goal alternatives and his repertoire

[10] Talcott Parsons, *The Structure of Social Action* (New York: McGraw-Hill, 1937).

of achievement methods are established by the cultural system of values and the social system of norms (expected ways of behaving) that are current in the social system of which he is a member.

That's it in a nutshell.

James Coleman   Coleman's most interesting and intriguing approach to the understanding of the nature of society or a "social system" utilizes the "gaming" or "game theory" or "game modeling" technique. This technique is sometimes referred to as "system simulation" when the game is played by computer. Essentially, it is an attempt to duplicate the major characteristics of social processes on a smaller, more easily observable scale.[11]

Hence, to simulate or to make a model of a social system, Coleman indicates two stages in this modeling process. First, a game is developed which one assumes will mirror the "dominant processes in a social system." (His is called the economic system game which, as it goes on, turns into the political system game—somewhat like monopoly except that moves are not made by the chance happenings of dice rolling.)

Second, a theory (or statement of what happens as the game is played) which describes how the game functions is developed. The games and the statements about the games represent what Coleman calls a "way station" between vague ideas and formal, scientific theory. The underlying assumptions of the game approach are essentially active-rational, and Coleman has been good enough to make his first assumptions very clear.

He begins by assuming that men are rational actors about whom we may assume nothing more than action being initiated and carried out for the purpose of achieving self-interests. Coleman realizes that this approach has its problems. (Just how much of human behavior is non-determined?) He also assumes that each player is determined to win, and that each player's definition of winning may be different. In other words, "goals are diverse." The diversity of goals along with a motivation to win has the

[11] James Coleman, "Game Models of Economic and Political Systems," in *The Study of Total Societies,* Samuel Klausner (Garden City, N. Y.: Doubleday, Anchor, 1967), pp. 30–44.

consequence of a by-product called "society" (order, rules, referees) which is based on this interdependence of the players (if players quit playing, nobody wins). Through the use of the game device, Coleman feels that abstract theory becomes simpler to develop.

Amitai Etzioni   As was indicated in Chapter 2, it is the author's belief that Etzioni's latest work, *The Active Society,* may have been written with the intention of showing the student of the turbulent sixties that there are effective modes of applying activity toward the ends of creating the "better society," short of mass behavior with its consequent violence and disorganizing effects. This is not to say that mass behavior cannot have positive effects for change, but rather, that this is not the time nor the place for its utilization. This might be a moot point to many readers, but be that as it may, Etzioni presents a very exhaustive analysis (from the action frame of reference) of the nature of power in sociological situations.

Etzioni's analysis pivots on the concept of "societal consciousness" or the actor's awareness of the situation.

> The more encompassing the consciousness of the actor, the more active he can be, because consciousness that is more encompassing increases the actor's options and frees him to act more in accord with his values and less in terms of environmental pressures and structural constraints. An actor who is aware of the malleability of his environment but not of the malleability of his own internal makeup foregoes a major set of options and limits his creativity. Similarly, an actor that is aware of the transformability of his environment and his body but not that of his guidance mechanisms excludes a whole range of options.[12]

From the author's point of view, it appears that Etzioni has begun with assumptions very similar to those of Parsons and has built upon these to develop a much more understandable and practical conceptualization of human action in the context of a

[12] Amitai Etzioni, *The Active Society* (New York: The Free Press, 1968), p. 36.

society. He then uses this as a basis for any program which is to be used in the establishment of an "authentic society."

> In the inauthentic society, the members are caught up in the typical cleavage between their private selves and public roles and manage by treating their neuroses with drugs, alcohol, professional counseling, and the like, thus reinforcing the inauthenticity of the society which caused their malaise. There is a minority of retreatists who ignore their public roles and build lives around their public selves. While these people are more authentic and potentially carriers of societal change, they have little societal effect. Finally, there are those who evolve new public selves which they collectivize and make the basis of their societal action. In these lies the hope for an initiation of the transformation of the inauthentic society. They are the active ones.[13]

The author interprets this to mean that the active man is the one who places his active, rational self prior to the determined, passive public role and with other active men seeks to bring into existence a society in which the self and the role are complementary.

---

[13] *Ibid.*, p. 65.

Chapter 4 Assumptions Employed in Social Explanation

ASSUMPTIONS OF MICROSOCIOLOGY The most basic assumptions on the microscopic level of explanation are those concerned with what might be referred to as animal needs and human wants. These are sometimes referred to in the literature as primary and secondary needs, or as basic needs and learned needs. The author will use the terms animal needs and human wants because these terms make the usage more straightforward. It is necessary that these be inventoried as the remainder of the assumptions and propositions in the text are derived or built upon them.

Animal Needs: Requisites for Survival To begin with, it should be understood that these animal needs are of a psychosomatic nature; they deal with things that are necessary for both biological survival and development and for emotional development. Such needs are generally considered to include the following:

1. Need for body contact and stimulation.
2. Need for fuel intake.
3. Need for activity.
4. Disposal of wastes.
5. The need for rest and relaxation.

It is assumed that without a minimum of contact between the mother and the infant the child will not develop properly either physiologically or mentally. In fact, the child would probably not survive. Such an assumption seems well supported by reports of feral children, isolated children, and research in stimulus deprivation.

Surely no one would question the assumption that a certain minimum amount of food, water, oxygen and trace elements must be ingested if the organism is to survive and grow.

It is further assumed that the human animal, as any animal, requires a certain amount of muscle activity and exercise for proper development and feelings of animal well-being. Such activity, it would appear, is also required for the proper removal of toxins and waste materials in the biological system and also for normal kinetic orientation.

These first three needs give rise to a fourth. It is assumed that the physiological system cannot survive unless waste products of the metabolic process are eliminated. Finally, it is assumed that the human organism requires periods of rest at which time the brain organizes the many stimuli impressed upon the nervous system, the cells rid themselves of toxins causing fatigue, and the system prepares itself for another period of need satisfaction. Among college students these periods of rest usually coincide with fifty-minute periods called "lectures."

Now then, taking all of these assumptions into account, along with the observation that human infants are unable to satisfy most of these without help, the necessity of a social organization becomes understandable. With the increasing complexity of several organisms linked interdependently as a society, some other kinds of needs arise which are directed at requisites concerned with things other than crass survival. These wants are group-centered and learned in interaction with other human organisms. They are no sooner satisfied than new ones arise and this makes them uniquely human wants.

The human animal is a peculiar beast.
His wanting is seldom ceased.

Anon.

Human Wants: The Societal Supermarket   The following assumptions have to do with wants which are the learned modifications and specializations or extensions of the animal needs. These wants may be listed as follows:

1. Extensions of body contact and stimulation needs.
2. Extensions of the food intake need.
3. Social extensions of activity and play needs.
4. Extensions of waste disposal needs.
5. Secondary extensions of the rest need.

It is assumed that the mother-infant contact and proto-erotic stimulation is extended to general gregariousness and group-centric behavior of the developing and mature human. Being a group member is an actively sought-after situation. Being liked by others is an assurance that human contact is not in jeopardy and gives one a certain sense of security. This leads to other more complex extensions of the contact need, such as the desire for status and prestige within the group setting. This will be covered at greater length later.

Another of the body contact extensions learned in group situations (parent-child, teacher-student) is that of sexual or erotic cathexis, which is to say we learn to specify certain types of physical contacts and stimulations that produce general enjoyment and have a tendency to desire repetition of such contacts whenever convenient. We also learn when it is convenient and when it is not.

Generally speaking, the learned extensions of the food intake need are referred to as taste. The old maxim which states that "there is no accounting for another man's taste" is fallacious. Man likes what he has been taught is tasty or good for him or enjoyable to eat. Moreover, the amount of food required to satisfy his hunger is to some degree a learned modification of the basic biological need. Socialized man wants certain kinds and a specified amount of food depending on his cultural context. This learned want necessitates that he and his societal associates must set up some system whereby these commodities may be produced and in the culturally defined amounts. Also, as groupings of men enlarge from tribes to complex societies, they must ever be creating systems whereby such commodities may be distributed.

Even among other mammals activity needs may be seen having their effects. Baboons play "tag" and "king of the mountain." House cats stalk imaginary prey and dogs in packs have mock dog fights. Some of this is, of course, triggered by genetic demands to practice survival techniques, but a good part of it appears to be just good fun. So it is among humans. Apart from the games which are specifically oriented toward mastering the techniques of being an adult, small children delight in just running pell-mell, or jumping, or fighting. It feels good to extend and stretch the muscles. A secondary modification of this is the institutionalization of forms of exertion generally referred to as sports, or athletics, or exercise. Generally speaking, these institutional forms of need expression combine the satisfaction of both body contacts—sexual and activity needs. Certain forms for the expression of these more complex of secondary wants are quite prevalent and are called parties. This particular form of need satisfaction fulfills a complex secondary want system of sexuality, food gorging, and dancing activity.

The organism does not need to learn how to dispose of body wastes, but the human must learn where and when this is to be done if he is going to maintain himself in good standing in the social group. Probably one of the first axioms to emerge was "There's a time and a place for everything." Man probably came to this realization as a result of the observation that the time was not during dinner and the place was not where he slept. The institutionalized form of establishing the locus of excretion was a simple chore for the primitive, but has become a complex technology for modern man living in crowded cities. Likewise, a good proportion of the time and training involved in transforming the infant organism into the adult human is devoted to the etiquette program of "where and when" regarding burping, flatulence, and excrement. So complex is this training in modern cultures that Freud based much of his psychology on it, indicating that deviations from what was practically necessary resulted in a whole host of emotional and personality difficulties.

Man also does not have to learn how to sleep or rest, but in the group situation he learns culturally prescribed patterns for when, how long, and where he sleeps. Most animals sleep or rest when they feel they need to, man sleeps when it is prescribed by his social grouping. This is probably the most dramatic example of how institutionalized forms may actually contradict biological well-being.

ASSUMPTIONS OF MACROSOCIOLOGY

Societal Requisites   These more macroscopic assumptions that we now want to deal with are concerned primarily with what must be done in order for individual needs to be met while maintaining the cohesiveness of the social group. Implicit is the assumption that human needs cannot be met without cooperative group activity, and, moreover, the group situation may possibly interfere with need satisfaction. These macroscopic requisites deal with assumptions relative to individual needs and wants being elaborated into group goals and societal preoccupations. These more macroscopic mechanisms that will now be dealt with are:

1. Division of labor.
2. Production of goods.
3. Distribution of goods.
4. Authority and legitimating patterns, or moral structures.

One of the most basic mechanisms operating to satisfy the dual necessity of individual wants and group goals is that of division of labor. The forms of this mechanism are quite varied. They vary from simple work-sharing patterns in small groups to complex occupational role structures in a complex society. These patterns are very utilitarian in their inception in that they are predicated by the desire to meet needs with an economy of time and energy expended. These work patterns serve very well the duality of group and individual in that they function to provide goods for consumption and also function to integrate the group. Group integration comes about when the various activities of the members are articulated in the cooperative effort of achieving group goals (shared individual goals). The following tableau illustrates this principle.

> As the scene opens a troop of manlike apes or maybe apelike men, women, and infants are gathered about a fire. Eyewitness TV takes you back to the dawn of history. Our hero, Og the lionlike, breaks the silence. "Hey gang, like I've got a plan. Man we gotta do something. We ain't gettin' enough grub, we're short on rest and the clubhouse smells. On top of all of that these screaming kids are driving me crazy." "Yea man, I can dig it," replies Munga longlegs. "It's a drag; first it's grub for roots, pull some kid out o'da swamp, run down a rabbit, pick up firewood, then grab some shuteye and start all over again." "Quit playing the martyr, Munga," says Lila lovely. "At least you don't have some kid on your breast while you're trying to run down the groceries, and those rabbits are fast, baby." Old one-eyed Dingo breaks in at this point. "This setup is bugging me, too; I can't walk through the camp without stepping in a pile of fresh oompah." "Well, here's what we're gonna do . . . ."

> And thus begins Og's plan. "We gotta get organized. For instance, you girls have a bit of a handicap chasing down game. Likewise those little handicaps drive me crazy alla time screamin'. We'll make a deal—you girls raise the kids—you're better at it—and us guys will do the hunting. Old Dingo here is gettin' too old to run so he can make slingshots and help with the younguns and we'll catch him a rabbit now and then. . . . Okay Ding', baby? Okay! And girls, as long as we'll be out chasing in the bush all day, why don't you fix up the campsight a little." I've been told that

the plan worked and they lived happily ever after . . .
would you believe a couple of years?

It can be seen that the division of labor mechanism was
necessitated by the need to maintain a food supply, rear the
young, make tools, and maintain the homesite in a manner which
was economical in regard to time and energy. As society increases in size (population) and complexity, it is increasingly
developing more involved forms of division of labor and produces
more varieties of goods and services. Also, more kinds of goods
and services are being demanded. The secondary wants become
more elaborate and quite removed from simple basic needs. The
satisfaction of such wants becomes the paramount activity of the
group (production) and of the individual (consumption). Man's
inventiveness and imagination is exceeded only by his appetite
and chronic dissatisfaction. The different labor divisions become
specialities and everyone becomes everyone else's patron.

Now here's where things get sticky. For instance, how many
of Og's rabbits are worth one of Dingo's slingshots? And who
makes that decision? Og is young and on his way to becoming
chief, while old Dingo is pretty thankful that they allow his rheu-
matic old bones around camp. Will Dingo get a fair shake?

If one can imagine problems such as this in a simple society,
how much more complex does this become in a modern, industrial society? The varied goods and services have to be exchanged and distributed in a more or less legitimate (if not
egalitarian) way. Exchanging a rabbit for a slingshot is simply
done. But how does one exchange a beefsteak for hooking up a
telephone? This requires a portable medium of exchange. Let's
try money. A piece of paper that essentially says, "I am worth four
pounds of beefsteak and/or a telephone hookup." Well, the exchange problem is solved, but how about the problem of how
many of what is worth how much of which? Who decides? Each
working society has to work this out. If it doesn't, the division of
labor breaks down and the production of goods falters.

For a number of reasons, once the systems have been established to satisfy the above three requisites, a fourth one is required, the purpose of which is to reinforce and maintain the

others. This fourth pattern maintains the legitimacy of the other three. On a nonmaterial level the patterns of division of labor, production of goods, and distribution of commodities are maintained and made legitimate by beliefs and values pervasive in the society and found in the religion, folklore, and myths of the society. On the physical or material level, this fourth pattern is observable in the religious rituals and organization, in the art, in the system of education, in the political organization, and in the written laws of the society. These legitimating beliefs or cultural traditions authorize the continuity of established social patterns and have the power of being moral dictums, the violations of which are either illegal, immoral, or treasonous. The power of moral sanction is not the only mechanism of legitimation. Through the school, the priesthood, and the family these society-maintaining values can be built into each newborn recruit to that society. The necessity for continual legitimating of the societal patterns derives from the fact that seldom do societies meet the first three requisites without some discrepancies. Which is to say, some people's needs are met better than others, especially when certain wanted commodities are scarce and/or there is a disjunction between the value of labor and the value of the goods produced.

STRUCTURES WHICH MEDIATE BETWEEN THE INDIVIDUAL AND HIS NEEDS AND BETWEEN SOCIETY AND ITS REQUISITES

Up to this point we have been talking about the two extremely different, yet mutually dependent, goal-attaining systems. At the microscopic extreme, it is the individual with his needs for maintaining a physiological and psychological existence. At the other extreme is the social macrocosm which evolves out of the collective goal attainment actions of individuals and develops needs or requisites of its own which must be met if the society is to operate and be maintained. The need now is for some mechanism which makes the macrocosm accessible to the individual and the microcosm available to the state. Such a mechanism is provided in the relations available to the individual in groups. Groups are social systems of person-to-person interaction which are intermediary in size and complexity in comparison to the individual and to the total society. Through the group or association, the individual has contact with his society and his culture. Likewise, through the group with its hold on the individual, the total society or the state has access to the individual. Through this mechanism, the demands for commitment to the requisites of society are impressed on the individual and the needs of the individual are conveyed to the state.

Groups are of many different types. Not only do they differ in size, but also in terms of the character of the relationships between the individuals in them. Generally speaking, groups and the nature of interpersonal relationships which characterize them are definable along a continuum between two polar types of group phenomena. At one extreme of the continuum is the polar group type which is referred to as the primary group.

At the other extreme of the continuum is the polar type group referred to as secondary. All real human groups can be characterized, then, in terms of how closely they approximate either of the two polar types. To show you how this works, let's first establish the dimensions of the two polar types and then look for examples of existing groups that range between these two polar abstractions.

A primary group is essentially one in which the relations between members are spontaneous and not a matter of ritual. Relations or interactions are face-to-face and intimate in an atmosphere of openness. Judgments of members' actions are dictated by each member's personal identity and personality rather than by society-wide standards of behavior.

On the other hand, the relationships in secondary groups are ritualized and rational or nonemotional. Interactions are impersonal and are status-to-status relations rather than person-to-person. Instead of openness, the atmosphere is one of intellectual closure and each member is judged on the basis of highly prescribed role expectations and his special personal traits carry no weight at all. Now, surely very few existing groups are of such a nature that they are identical to the ideal types that were just defined. But they approximate these types to the extent that some groups are practically primary and some are practically secondary, and we can differentiate between them on the basis of how close they come to the ideals. For instance, in the following diagram, would you place these groups on the line that goes from primary to secondary: a family, a PTA group, an industrial corporation, a bridge club, a barbershop quartet, the president's cabinet, a coffee klatch?

The Primary-Secondary Continuum

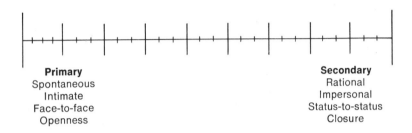

Primary	**Secondary**
Spontaneous	Rational
Intimate	Impersonal
Face-to-face	Status-to-status
Openness	Closure

You aren't sure? That's understandable. We're not positive either. Perhaps when you have finished this book you can come back and place these groups on the continuum with a little more sophistication. This is one of the issues we will be addressing in the following pages. Later, when the author refers to the bureaucracy of a corporation as a group characterized by secondary relations, you will know what that means. But let's get back to the idea that groups function to mediate between the individual and his society and his culture. There are some concepts that must be defined in order that this discussion might continue in a fruitful manner. To be specific, there are certain mechanisms in the group's phenomena that make up the basic machinery of this mediation function.

The Mechanisms of Mediation: The Dynamics of Status and Role
In everyday observation, groups are made up of people, but in reality they are comprised of things that are not immediately observable. These are things abstracted from observing groups and the particular way in which people react and interact with each other within these groups. Two such things—mechanisms of the ongoing group process—are referred to as statuses and roles.

A status is a position in a group or social organization. The several statuses make up the structure of a group. For instance, a baseball team is a highly contrived group. The several co-ordinated statuses or positions are pitcher, catcher, first baseman, shortstop, etc. In a group called the family, the positions or statuses are father, mother, and child. All of these are abstract positions into which any number of individuals may be "plugged" at one time or over a long period.

A role is a pattern of behavior which is prescribed for or expected of a particular person who is occupying a specific status in the group. For instance, when Mr. A occupies the status of catcher in the baseball team, certain behaviors are expected of him, behaviors different from all others concerned. Should he deviate from these, he may be shifted to left field or sent to the showers or fined by the umpire. He may even find himself kicked off the team with Mr. B placed in the status of catcher. Likewise, if Mr. C does not fulfill certain role prescriptions while occupying the status of father and husband in the family group, he may find himself in the doghouse, in divorce court, or chased by the sheriff for nonsupport. Or, on the other hand, he may react in some negative fashion to Mrs. C if she fails to play the role of mother-wife correctly. The cohesion of the group, then, is maintained by the reciprocal nature of the role expectations attached to each of the statuses.

Now then, how does one get into a status? Sociologists generally recognize two processes of occupying statuses. The first is by ascription; the second by achievement. If a person occupies a status by ascription it is meant that he is in that position through no choice of his own. Either he was born into that status, or he was placed there by the group, or by traditional norms in that status. On the other hand, if a person occupies a status by achievement, it is meant that he has, by his actions, acquired the specific traits, identity characteristics, or role performance abilities which allow him to compete and subsequently achieve occupancy of that status.

Chapter 5 The Small and the Primary Group: Focus of Socialization and Problem Solving

We have noted earlier that individuals require the presence of other individuals doing their specialized tasks in order to survive. In other words, we need others who play roles which complement ours. The newborn child requires someone to play the role fulfilling the specialized task of mother, or it will not survive during its first years of extreme dependence. But even after the child has grown to a point where it might possibly see to its own physical survival, there still exists a requirement for others to provide emotional reinforcements and training (socialization of a continuing nature) for the ever new and complex roles that the individual plays at each stage of his development.

The type of group situation which best fits the requirements of nurturing the new recruit to society is the primary group. This type of group is one in which relations between people are usually characterized by face-to-face interaction and personal relationships are an end in themselves rather than a means to the arbitrary goals of an individual member. The family represents one of these groups. Although the most salient in regard to the earliest stages of the individual's development, the family is by no means the only source of primary relations and socialization.

Berelson and Steiner indicate that there are four general types of primary groups.

> (1) The autonomous group, e.g., a circle of close friends built on free choice and voluntary association; (2) the institutionalized small group, e.g., the family; (3) the small group within a large organization, often called a mediating group because of its linking position between the individual and the organization, e.g., the work group in a factory or office, a group of soldiers (buddies) in the army; and (4) the problem-solving group, e.g., a committee with a task to perform.[1]

They go on to argue that those groups which are institutionalized (family and work groups) share values because they have close contact. Free association groups are comprised of people who choose contact because they share values.[2] This becomes an important characteristic distinction as we explore how the group socializes the individual and provides him with certain survival and emotional needs or means of solving various problems.

The Family: An Institutionalized Group   It is often said in jest that people deserve what they get in life because they didn't choose their parents. This statement points out only too well that one of the most important group situations in our lives is one over which we had no choice. Most of us may be thankful that we were lucky in this regard while others find little comfort in the idea that they are partially blameless for their lot in life. At any rate, one cannot overemphasize the importance of the family (à la adults and children in a primary setting) with regard to the molding of attitudes, values, and traits which mark the socialized individual.

---

[1] Bernard Berelson, and Gary A. Steiner, *Human Behavior* (New York: Harcourt Brace Jovanovich, 1964), p. 326.

[2] *Ibid.,* p. 327.

At birth the individual is ascribed the status of child and placed in the care of a specified adult and/or a number of adults who face the task of nurturing the child with a variety of notions and ideas about the intended end product of their nurturing. Likewise, the idea of how important the nurturing role is will vary from one adult socializer to the next.

Socialization is the process whereby the individual learns techniques and acquires traits which enable him to achieve adult statuses and play the concomitant roles. He also learns about those statuses toward which he may realistically aspire. He acquires the attitudes and values which form his personality and the rudiments for eventually starting his own family and becoming a socializer himself.

Obviously, the role of the family group is more than the socialization of the child, and, of course, the role of the family changes from time to time and from place to place. Needless to say, the biological roles of reproduction for father and mother are pretty well fixed, but fulfilling the social role of father or mother can be, and often is, accomplished by persons other than the biological parents.

In some societies it has been observed that a maternal uncle takes on most of the role obligations that are accomplished by the individual called father in our society. In other societies (and in some regions of our own society) family means a host of assorted kin—grandparents, uncles, aunts, cousins, nieces, nephews; however, it is becoming the rule in our society that family means father, mother, and child.

The terms used to differentiate between these two types of families are "extended family" for the former and "nuclear" for the latter. Most often the extended family is associated with an agricultural or preindustrial society, while the nuclear family is associated with the mobility, secularism, and complexity of a modern industrial society. Along with this shift from the extended to the nuclear family in the transition to industrialism there is also a shift in the role of the family in society and the role of individuals in the family.

Initially, the family was the all-pervasive social institution. Its role was that of the basic economic productive unit, the educator of children, the protector of the aged, etc. In contemporary industrial society, the family functions less in these regards and most of these functions are becoming the priority of the state. The socializing influence of the parents is minimized after age six, when the child attends school. Similarly, the responsibilities for the aged patriarchs and matriarchs of the family no longer fall upon the shoulders of the eldest son, but rather upon the state's social security and society's homes for the aged.

It appears that the role of the family becomes less and less over time, but the importance of the remaining functions increases tremendously. Early socialization and emotional reinforcements are the salient functions of the contemporary nuclear family. As society becomes marked more and more by the secondary relations of the job and the marketplace in the rationalization of economic life, it becomes apparent that the family may be one of the few sources of intensely primary relations for both the adults and children involved. This observation has been put forth as one trial explanation for the high rate of divorce in industrial states. Briefly put, if the family is the source for the satisfaction of very primary needs, individuals not finding satisfaction in the only place they could hope to find it will seek out another primary relationship. This may help to explain why very young marriages, numerous other marriages, and the recent trend toward trial marriage are gaining popularity among university and college students. It is, in short, the quest for primary relationships in a sea of secondariness.

The Problem-Solving Group: Somewhat Institutionalized   It should be remembered that the terms "forced" and "free" regarding association are relative terms. A point is made of this, because the reader may find it puzzling that the author considers the problem-solving group as a somewhat institutionalized group of rather forced associations. It is so considered simply because the nature of such a group is to solve a specific task which requires specific individuals who have specific talents. Some texts refer to such associations as "duty calls." These groups are not so spontaneous and primary as are the voluntary small group associations. In fact, because of the specific role traits required for the statuses in these situations, they border on being secondary groups. However, they are small groups, and relations are face-to-face. Also, the problem-solving aspect requires intimate and free exchange which, therefore, necessitates a certain level of primariness.

Examples of such groups include committees, boards, task forces, and so-called "think tanks." They may occur in the context of larger, secondary, bureaucratic organizations, but for the period of their generally transitory existence they are outside the bounds of bureaucratic rules. They are primary, but generally not completely voluntary associations.

Generally speaking, for purposes of efficiency or brainstorming, depending on the nature of their task, such groups will organize themselves accordingly. Task-oriented groups with specific problems and short deadlines will select a leader or chairman (or one will emerge), and a fixed or structured pattern of communication will emerge after a time. Where the nature of the problem is somewhat undefined and group morale is a prime requirement, the group may remain more unstructured with open communication being the rule.

The extent of efficiency in such patterns was demonstrated by Alex Bavelas as early as 1950. His concern was to study the effects of different communication patterns in problem-solving groups of five persons each. Four types of group communication patterns were developed. Five subjects were recruited for each group type and each group was given the same problem to solve. Obviously, such controlled laboratory settings are going to be different from the real settings of task-oriented groups as far as members, problems, environment, etc. are concerned. Yet, even with this limitation, the findings of Bavelas shed light on the nature of such groups and the utility of specific communication structures.[3] Following is a diagram of the four communication structures. Arrows indicate the paths of communication.

Each subject had a card bearing five geometric symbols. One symbol was common to all five subjects' cards. The task was to find out which design was common to all of the five subjects. They

[3] Alex Bavelas, "Communications Patterns in Task-Oriented Groups," *Acoustical Society of America,* XXII (1950), pp. 725–730.

The Circle

Each person communicates to his left and to his right. A can talk to B and E, B can talk to A and C, etc.

The Line

A and E can talk to only one other person. B, C and D can talk to both neighbors.

The Star

Only E can talk to all of the other four. A, B, C, and D can talk only to E.

The "Y"

C can talk with A, B, and D. A, B, and E can talk to only one person. D can talk to both C and E.

were timed for the speed of solving the problem and the errors were counted. The subjects were questioned afterward relative to their general morale.

Bavelas found that the Y pattern generated the lowest errors and exhibited the quickest solution to the problem. The central position in the Y emerged as the leader due to his greater access to communication. The Star and the Line patterns were next in efficiency, while the Circle pattern generated the most errors and required the most time for the solution of the problem. This pattern, however, exhibited the highest group morale. The Star and Line were second in morale and the Y was lowest in morale. Generally speaking, persons in central positions had the greatest satisfaction. One would, therefore, assume that persons with the most chances for communication were the most satisfied. One important aspect of the research was the observation that after successive trials the Circle group developed leadership and technique which facilitated an increase in efficiency while high morale was maintained.

Autonomous Groups: Peer Groups   In the reader's experience, small groups of free association will probably emerge as the most obvious group type next to the family. So common are they to our experience that we are only seldom conscious of their structure and patterning. Earlier we discussed reference groups and their effect upon the motivation of group members. It is especially the family and peer groups which serve the purpose of reference groups in our social and psychological lives. Both groups provide the intense, intimate interaction necessary to mold attitudes and to reinforce behavior, one by a long, forced association, and the other by virtue of the choice of association with others whose association we desire or which is available to us either by their proximity or because of their similarity to ourselves or our needs. Peer groups are represented by associations such as fraternities, sororities, adolescent gangs, street corner society, neighborhood cliques, bridge clubs, coffee klatches, ad infinitum. Popular literature ranging from the *Bowery Boys* to stories of suburban intrigue recount numerous episodes of this phenomenon in human existence, and friendship itself appears to be a high priority concern in popular literature.

Two good descriptions of autonomous peer groups are available to us in sociological literature—a description of adolescent gangs by Frederic Thrasher[4] and a study of street corner society by William Whyte.[5]

[4] Frederic M. Thrasher, *The Gang* (Chicago: University of Chicago Press, 1927).
[5] William F. Whyte, *Street Corner Society* (Chicago: University of Chicago Press, 1943).

Thrasher's study of 1,100 boys' gangs in the Chicago slums of the 1920s has become a classic bit of sociological literature. The major portion of the gangs studied (895) were small groups (under 20 members) and were, in every respect, primary groups. The larger gangs were really federations of smaller groups; so, in general, all the groups functioned as primary groups. Thrasher indicated that the primary, face-to-face relations and the emotional closeness of the members were the chief purposes of the gangs for the members. The gang provided, in other words, an almost familial association for adolescents to whom family situations were less than optimum.[6]

To say that a group is primary does not mean, however, that it has no structure and no role differentiation. Thrasher pinpointed distinct roles in the structure of the gang and several types of leaders. The special role-status designations which may emerge in such gangs were reported in the gang argot by Thrasher as: "The brains, the jester, the sissy, the show-off, and the goat."[7] Each played a significant role and each occupied a significant position in the status hierarchy. Leadership was diffused among a number of personalities who would bring their special abilities, knowledge, or craft to the fore when the particular situation called for it.

Thrasher noted a very democratic nature in the gangs. The leaders had to accommodate themselves to gang wishes. To make a mistake in this manner meant loss of power and influence. Social control in the groups was generally maintained by the subtle forces of group opinion. Although physical punishment was sometimes utilized, it was secondary to the coercion of group pressure or the threat of loss of group membership or status.

William F. Whyte's analysis of a few gang situations in Boston's Italian community was not as extensive as the number of gangs observed, but was extensive in the depth to which Whyte became acquainted with and described one gang in particular, "The Nortons." Whyte's in-depth research of the Nortons began, and was greatly facilitated by, the happenstance of meeting and befriending their leader, "Doc." Involvement with the gang as

[6] Thrasher, *op. cit.*, pp. 288–328.
[7] *Ibid.*, p. 326.

Doc's friend gave Whyte the opportunity for an inside look at a voluntary peer group in action.

The Nortons were a group in which members of various abilities, capacities, and talents were joined together in unified activity. With Doc at the top, a position hard won, the rest of the group was arranged in a descending hierarchy of power and influence.

The Structure of the Nortons [8]

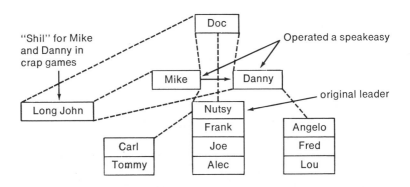

Doc, Mike, and Danny were the most influential of the group because of either physical prowess or contacts beyond the world of the street corner. They were the cosmopolitans, so to speak. Generally, decisions were made at the top and then passed down through the ranks, although information was always solicited from all members during any planning sessions. Above all, the group functioned for each member as an end in itself—a mutually satisfying experience.

The Mediating Group As was mentioned before, the mediating group is a smaller primary entity within a larger secondary organization. It is referred to as a mediating group because, although primary and spontaneous, it links the individual to the organization by counteracting the coldness of the bureaucratic structure. While it may function in a way contradictory to the formal goals of

[8] Adapted from Whyte, *op. cit.*

efficiency and formal policy, it may also function to increase efficiency by establishing channels of communication and procurement. Although these channels may not be consistent with bureaucratic procedure, they may hasten the attainment of organizational goals while simultaneously providing primary ties for the people in question.

The phenomenon of the informal group within the formal organization is described in an article by Donald Roy written in the mid-fifties.[9] Roy reports observations made while working as a machine operator in a factory. Some of his most interesting observations deal with the development of informal procedures for the establishment and meeting of production quotas by primary work groups on the production line. The main implication of his description is that the norms of primary groups have at times more control over the worker than do managerial dictates from on high.

Group norms define a fair day's work, proper work procedure, and a chain of influence, all of which, or a part of which, may be in direct contradiction to the formal definitions of managerial policy. The salience of informal group norms are impressed upon even certain representatives of management such as foremen. These informal group norms served the functions of allowing workers to increase the control of their work environment, lessening their dependence on management, and assuring the meeting of common worker objectives. They increased the job security of workers because they limited production to save work for "rainy days" or times of production slowdown. They also strengthened group solidarity and controlled competition among workers.[10]

Sanctions for those who violate informal group norms are rather stringent in the mediating group situation. These also aid in maintaining the primary cohesion of the informal group, a latent effect of which is less worker turnover and higher productivity in the long run.[11]

[9] Donald Roy, "Efficiency and the Fix: Informal Intergroup Relations in a Piecework Machine Shop," *American Journal of Sociology*, LX (November, 1954), pp. 255–266.

[10] *Ibid.*

[11] Berelson, and Steiner, *op. cit.*, pp. 408–409.

The Small Group Model   What kinds of things are common to all small groups, and, what kinds of things must be present to make the group interaction effective or successful in meeting varied group goals? Clovis Shepherd affords us some answers in the conclusion of his book on small groups.[12] He presents a model that delimits the essential features of a successfully operating small group. His statement gives us a general rule, an ideal type, something by which we may assess any existent group. Moreover, the model ties together our discussion at this point and allows us to see what kinds of things are universal to small group behavior.

Shepherd indicates that there are at least five features common to all groups, and, when the five features occur in specified ways, the probability of a successful group experience is high. These features in outline are:

1. *Objectives*
   a. A successful group has clear objectives (goals).
   b. Member objectives of a successful group are the same or are compatible with those of the group.
   c. The more time needed for clarification of objectives, the less time there is for achieving them.

2. *Role Differentiation*
   a. For group success each member's role is clear and known to himself and to the group.
   b. For group success the member roles should also be clear in terms of prestige grades of the statuses.

3. *Values and Norms*
   a. "A group in which members do not share at least some relevant values is likely to be successful only for limited and short-run objectives."
   b. Some differences in values may be tolerated but very little difference in norms can be tolerated.
   c. "In a successful group, norms of various types are clear and agreed upon." "Action occurs through consensus, not through majority vote or minority railroading."

[12] Clovis Shepherd, *Small Groups: Some Sociological Perspectives* (San Francisco: Chandler Press, 1964), pp. 122–125.

4. *Membership*

   a. "Membership in a successful group is clear-cut and the members are heterogeneous."
   b. Diverse skills, experience, and interest are factors which encourage role differentiation and flexibility in functioning.

5. *Communication*

   a. In a successful group, communication is open and full.
   b. No *relevant* information is withheld (ideas or feelings).
   c. *But,* information is provided only when it is appropriate.
   d. Information that might cause disruption is by definition not relevant and is withheld.

Generally speaking, when these five process features are met in the ways outlined we would expect the observation of a successful group—one which is cohesive, productive, and autonomous. The following passage from Steinbeck's *Tortilla Flat* exemplifies such a relationship.

> "We must take this money to Danny."
> Their first appetite over, they were sipping the wine out of fruit jars now.
> "What is the great need Danny has for two dollars?" Jesus Maria asked.
> Pilon grew confidential. His hands came into play like twin moths, restrained only by his wrists and arms from flying out the door.
> "Danny our friend is taking up with Mrs. Morales. Oh, I don't think Danny is a fool. Mrs. Morales has two hundred dollars in the bank. Danny wants to buy a box of big candy for Mrs. Morales."
> "Candy is not good for people," Pablo observed. "It makes their teeth ache."
> "That is up to Danny," said Jesus Maria. "If he wants to ache Mrs. Morales teeth, that is his business. What do we care for Mrs. Morales teeth?"
> A cloud of anxiety had settled on Pilon's face. "But," he interposed sternly, "if our friend Danny takes

big candy to Mrs. Morales, he will eat some, too. So it is the teeth of our friend that will ache."

Pablo shook his head anxiously. "It would be a bad thing if Danny's friends, on whom he depends, should bring about the aching of his teeth."[13]

The reader will recall how this small group with shared values and clear-cut norms solved the problem of Danny's two dollars. They bought two gallons of wine, saved Danny's teeth, and thus had some good fortune for which to put the wine to good use.

[13] John Steinbeck, *Tortilla Flat* (New York: Viking Press, 1963), p. 27.

Chapter 6 The Stratification of Roles and the Development of Social Classes

If it is a biological fact that all men are created equal, it is also a biological fact that equality stops at the moment of conception. Likewise, it is also a fact that all men live in inequality in one or more dimensions of their social life. Though political systems of an enlightened variety seek sincerely to give all men equality before the law (a condition not yet reached in reality), men have never been equals in the marketplace. Material things as well as immaterial prestige and esteem are commodities which are differentially competed for and differentially allocated. There always exists some rationale for systems of allocation and distribution. To describe these systems, to report the rationale, and to explain their operation is the study of social stratification. It is the author's purpose to present the basic concepts and concerns which explain to some degree the phenomenon of classes.

It is important that the reader keep in mind the concepts of societal requisites, group membership, roles and statuses, the socialization process, and concepts dealing with human needs which have been introduced earlier, as these are important to the understanding of social stratification.

To begin with, for what kinds of activities would the group reward the individual? Logically, it would appear that the group rewards behavior that is perceived as conducive to the achievement of group and individual member's goals. Individuals who are personally instrumental in the acquisition of the shared goals of the group are going to receive the admiration and esteem of other group members. (That is, if the others see this behavior as being utilitarian, or define it as such.)

The question can then be raised, how will the group reward the individual? Rewards will be in the form of goods and prestige. So we begin by noting that actions are rewardable on the basis of shared values and definitions of the group. Sometimes, however, the action need not occur in order that the group's rewards be achieved. Individuals who possess the qualities and traits deemed necessary for the accurate completion of group-valued actions receive esteem and prestige as a kind of retainer against such time as the actions will be required.

Likewise, rewards in the form of material possessions, as they accumulate, become the symbols of what is perceived as earned esteem, and possession of these status symbols is at times sufficient for continued group respect.

Even at the level of the smaller group or tribe one can appreciate the complexities of the ranking of statuses, which is initially accomplished on the utilitarian level of rewardable action and later on the expressive action of rewardable qualities and possessions.

Stratification becomes much more complex as one shifts the focus of attention from the stratification of roles in the face-to-face group, to the stratification of classes of people in total society. And, as the concurrent shift from group influence to political power becomes an added concern, it is evident that such a topic becomes a semester's course all by itself. The author will attempt only to sketch the highlights of this concern, as volumes have been devoted to all of its complexities and digressions.

Concern with the existence, nature, and consequences of social classes and differing kinds of stratification systems is an ancient concern. Aristotle was intrigued by the problem of how the fate of the city-state was related to the relative preponderance and power of any one of three classes of citizens. He believed the state was composed of three classes which were stratified primarily according to economics and material possessions: the rich, the poor, and the mean or middle class. He distrusted both the poor and the rich classes because he felt that a preponderance of either led to negative political consequences for the state. The rich tended toward roguery and intrigue, and the poor tended toward thievery. The middle class, on the other hand, was the backbone of the state and the locus of responsible legislators.

Political ascendency of the rich led to oligarchy, the political ascendency of the poor led to democracy (what we mean today by hyper-democracy or anarchy), and the political ascendency of the middle class resulted in stable republican representation. The implication was that the middle classes were concerned with justice, unlike the other two classes who were thought to be concerned only with personal wealth. Moreover, Aristotle anticipated certain demographic principles when he indicated that the larger city-states would have the best government because there the middle class would outnumber the other extremes.

Such a clean trichotomy is seldom found or anticipated by contemporary sociologists in their identification of the class systems of modern industrial societies. Nor are such simplistic explanations given for the motivations, economic or otherwise, of individuals involved. Aristotle was speculating on the basis of his limited experience and from his perspective gained from the sphere of Greek life in which he existed. His response to the nature of classes of men was an existential and subjective response. This does not diminish the genius of Aristotle or any of the speculations that followed him in subsequent centuries of speculations. It simply points to the inadequacies of speculation based on limited observations.

It is not until the nineteenth century that such speculation reached its apex in the economic determinism of Karl Marx and was followed a century later by elaborate research methods and critical investigation seeking to objectify the nature of status hierarchies in human behavior.

To explain stratification on the basis of economics alone was philosophically intriguing, but it was not scientifically satisfactory, for it left many questions unanswered and it presupposed that all men were economically conscious and, hence, economically motivated. Such a claim demands proof, a kind of proof that logical inquiry is not sufficient to provide. Such speculation, however, serves its function in a developing science, inasmuch as it asserts propositions which require evidence, and in so doing, generate the hypotheses of those who demand to be shown. As astrology gave birth to astronomy, alchemy gave birth to chemistry, and religion to psychoanalysis, so did Hegel's and Marx's speculation give birth to more skeptical and more scientific approaches to the nature of class, status, and power.

The Sociology of Karl Marx   The idea that the economic factor of social life has great effect on all other aspects of society was not original with Karl Marx. Sorokin points out that such an idea was central to the writings of the ancient oriental and occidental historians and continued to be of concern among historians and philosophers up to and including the contemporaries of Marx. Likewise, this concern is still present among contemporary philosophers, historians, and sociologists.[1]

Confucius indicated how poverty creates much dissatisfaction and disorder, concluding that a satisfactory economic life is necessary for an orderly society. Buddha noted that "around hunger and love is centered the whole history of mankind." And, Aristotle, whom we have remarked about earlier, felt that the "causes for which men will be seditious are profit and honor. . . . To avoid dishonor or loss of fortune . . . they will raise a commotion in the state."[2]

But aside from this, Marx's argument for the deterministic nature of the economic factor on all other aspects of society is the

[1] Pitirim Sorokin, *Contemporary Sociological Theories* (New York: Harper, Torchbooks, 1964).

[2] *Ibid.*, p. 515.

first thorough, forceful, and most complete statement of this hypothesis.

Because our concern here is mainly with the *sociology* of Karl Marx vis-à-vis the nature of social class, there are two basic notions in his work which, along with some associated ideas, provide us with real contributions to the understanding of classes in society. Nicholas Timasheff indicates that, "As sociological theory, Marxism is reducible to two basic postulates and a few corollaries."[3]

Postulate I   The economic factor is the fundamental determinant of the structure and development of society. Here is how the argument goes. The technological means of production bring into existence the social organization of production (the nature of relationships between people enveloped in the productive activity). This occurs independently of human will. As means, men, materials, products, and markets are drawn into relation, the organization of production shapes the whole superstructure of society. Technological means then shape the nature of politics, laws, religion, philosophy, art, literature, science, and morality.

Postulate II   The second postulate is concerned with the nature of historical process or social change. Social change must be understood in terms of three ever-present phases through which the order proceeds. All orders of society pass through the "three stages of affirmation, or thesis, negation or antithesis, and reconciliation or synthesis." The process then begins again as the new order has as its affirmation the synthesis of the preceding process.

Combining postulates I and II and adding to this some observations of human history, the following corollaries are derived and represent the essence of Marx's critique of capitalism, his notion of the development of social classes, and his predictions for a social utopia.

The system of economic production and its consequent social

---

[3] Nicholas Timasheff, *Sociological Theory* (New York: Random, 1967), p. 49.

organization began as an affirmation. It was the best system and the most applicable order for the time. Such was capitalism at the onset of the industrial revolution which supplanted the medieval order of Europe. But the affirmation soon became an obstacle to new technological advances, new markets, and new sources of material which are now the negation or antithesis. A new order of production arose out of the conflicting thesis and antithesis and became a reconciliation of certain aspects of each. It was then the affirmation and the process continued.

It is in relation to this dialectic that Marxian notions of class are most understandable. For Marx there always existed two classes, each of which represented the social organization associated with one aspect of the dialectical process. One class represented the obsolete affirmation, the other the new order latent in the negation. Therefore, in the medieval stage of history, aristocracy represented the obsolete affirmation and the bourgeoisie represented negation, and the outcome was capitalism, in which the bourgeoisie became the affirmation and the proletariat the negation. The outcome of the industrial dialectic, Marx predicted, would be a classless society, at which time the dialectical process would end in the socialist utopia. Marx indicated that the final revolution would occur when the proletariat representing the negation becomes conscious of itself, i.e., the proletarians become class conscious and join together in unions and organizations to wrest the means of production, the products, and the authority for their distribution from the bourgeoisie.

The above is a much simplified account of Marxist economics and sociology, but it does represent the essence of Marx, which has had great impact on economics and sociology of the twentieth century. The impact of Marx is noted in that American and European sociology of stratification has been for the most part represented by theory and research aimed at an attempt either to test and verify these hypotheses, or to put them down once and for all.

Stratification Research and Theory in Twentieth Century Sociology
Berelson and Steiner in chapter eleven of *Human Behavior* began their coverage of stratification in a way which implicitly takes it out of the realm of purely monistic economic determinism.

Who and what are classified? People are put into classes by other people in the society, but the determination is only seldom made individual by individual, as is true, for example, in the case of purely moral judgements. Instead, the classifying judgements are typically based on conventional criteria that distinguish broad social groups (such as immigrants, the rich, the educated); or the members of organizations or institutions (such as college faculties, government employees, army officers).[4]

They then go on to list the dimensions from which criteria are developed, the result of which are the bases for the classification of peoples and the stratification of society. Observe in this list that these dimensions refer to roles, roles that are related to either utilitarian economic behavior or to expressive qualitative traits or characteristics.

1. Authority.
2. Power (political, economic, military).
3. Ownership of property, relation to the means of production, control of land (feudal estates).
4. Income—amount, type, sources.
5. Consumption patterns and style of life.
6. Occupation or skill and achievement in it.
7. Education, learning, wisdom.
8. Divinity, control over the supernatural.
9. Altruism, public service, morality.
10. Place in "high society"—kinship connections, ancestry, i.e., inherited position.
11. Associational ties and connections.
12. Ethnic status, religion, race.

It should be observed that these dimensions are not mutually exclusive, which is to say, any one of them cannot be considered singly in that all of these dimensions are related. Amount of income affects the amount of education and vice versa. Power re-

---

[4] Bernard Berelson, and Gary A. Steiner, *Human Behavior* (New York: Harcourt Brace Jovanovich, 1964), p. 454.

sides in ownership of property and associational ties. Likewise, the importance of these dimensions as bases for classification differs from country to country and from region to region. In some societies the dimension of race may negate the other eleven dimensions. However, when these dimensions are weighted and applied, stratification systems are distinguishable and the resulting descriptions lead to a more precise understanding of the stratification phenomenon.

It must be remembered, however, that not only are people evaluated and classed in social systems, but, likewise, the dimensions used are ranked and evaluated relative to their salience from culture to culture; for example, occupations are classed in ranks and holders of occupational positions are then subject to an evaluation based partly on the relative prestige of the occupational position they hold.

Man is committed to social or group life as the means by which he attempts to satisfy both his biological needs and the real or imagined needs that arise out of group life itself.[5] Within this social or group life, persons act out various roles that have been established by the group to the end that the goals of the group may be achieved. In view of the interdependent character of role relationships and the importance attached by group members to appropriate performance of role expectations, persons within the group are more or less constantly evaluated in terms of their relation to the system and to the other persons who comprise it.

For the part they play in the achievement of the goals of the group, members expect certain kinds of rewards. Rewards are limited, however, in relation to the demand for them. As a consequence, some system of reward allocation develops. In utopian conceptions of society such a system of allocation may be based upon a principle of complete equality among the members of the group. In reality, rewards are allocated differentially, usually in

---

[5] Material dealing with ranking and role behavior has been drawn from the following sources: Talcott Parsons, "A Revised Analytical Approach to the Theory of Social Stratification," pp. 93–128, and Pitirim Sorokin, "What Is Social Class?" pp. 87–92 in *Class, Status and Power*, eds. Reinhard Bendix, and Seymour Martin Lipset (Glencoe, Ill.: The Free Press, 1953). R. Freedman, A. H. Hawley, W. Landecker, G. E. Lenski, and H. Miner, *Principles of Sociology* (New York: Holt, Rinehart and Winston, 1956), pp. 231–249.

terms of the relative importance of the roles that are played by group members. Societal definitions of such role relationships constitute an important part of the normative system of the group. The specific bases upon which the group allocates rewards are sometimes referred to as rank systems. A rank system refers to a series of positions along a vertical hierarchy of some significant aspect of group life. Occupation, education, race, and athletic prowess serve as bases for some of the rank systems of our society. In each of these rank systems some positions are rated higher by group members than other positions. Thus, in our society, the banker is rated higher than the plumber, the college graduate is rated higher than the high school graduate, "whites" are rated higher than "nonwhites," and the baseball player of a major league team is rated higher than a member of the local sandlot team.

In addition to the differential evaluation of the positions in rank systems, societal members assign differential values to the various rank systems themselves. Educational position, for example, might be viewed as being more important in our society than is a hunting or fishing skill. On the other hand, a hunting or fishing skill might be viewed as being more important than poker-playing ability.

The significance of these considerations for the individual member of the group stems from the fact that each person occupies some position within each of several rank systems. All of the rank positions of a person, taken together and in terms of the relative importance of each, determines the status of the individual within the social system. This status, in turn, determines the amount of reward allocated to that individual by the group.

In general, any system of ranking of group members in terms of status may be termed social stratification. The particular form that the stratification system takes will vary from society to society and from time to time. The significant fact of social life is that some form of stratification tends to occur in every social system.

Stratification systems vary from one society to another in at least two major respects: (1) the aspects of behavior that make up the specific rank systems, together with the ordering of rank systems by group members, and (2) the ease with which group members of any given status are able to move to another status category. The latter factor refers, of course, to the phenomenon known as vertical or social mobility.

Stratification systems that permit considerable movement from one status to another are usually referred to as *class* systems of stratification; those that tend to discourage or prohibit movement from one status level to another are termed *caste* systems. The term *social class* refers to all the persons of the same or similar status in a class system of stratification; the term *caste* refers to all the persons of the same or similar status in a caste system of stratification.

It should be noted here that while the terminology used is suggestive of discrete differences between the two systems, the systems actually tend to be continuous. It is also possible to have both caste-like and class-like features within a single society. In the United States, for example, the overall system tends to be class-like, but evidence of caste-like features are seen in some relations involving Negroes and whites.

It would appear (judging from the basis of American literary content) that there is a cultural value placed on movement within the class system of the United States. There seems to be a widespread belief in this country that mobility upward through the strata of society and achievement of new status is possible for anyone who would strive for it. Needless to say, there is some basis for that belief, as it is often possible to move from one rank to another. And, in comparison with other industrial nations, our societal class structure is relatively open. This is not to say, however, that we have achieved the ideal open system.

On the other hand, vestiges of a caste-like structure do remain in certain regions. Previously, the door to mobility and achievement was closed to nearly all minority ethnic groups in our society. Today those people who carry the visible characteristics of their ethnic heritage (usually skin color) are still locked in the grip of ascribed status and a caste-like class position.

There has been some progress in recent years. The ethic of ability over parentage appears to be winning out when one hears statements like, "I don't care what a man's color is; as long as he has the abilities to do the job, I'll hire him." One major minority group yet remains in a definitely caste-like position—those persons without the acquired abilities, as the uneducated. Unfortunately, one often finds that the opportunity for education is closely linked to ethnic status. Until ethnic minorities are provided a greater opportunity for educational advancement, latent caste-like characteristics will still exist in American society.

Social mobility on the part of any group member is dependent upon his ability to acquire the distinguishing characteristics of a status other than the one he presently occupies.[6] This means that the member must alter his position in one or more of the important rank systems of his society. There is general agreement that occupational position, educational achievement, and income category are among the most important rank systems in the United States. Each of these rank systems is, of course, considerably dependent upon each of the others. Thus, higher educational achievement may be a prerequisite to a higher occupational position which, in turn, is associated with a higher income category.

Other means of movement within the structure are possible, however, and must be recognized in any thoroughgoing study of stratification phenomena. Since status is usually assigned to family units rather than to the individual per se, and since the wife is ascribed the position of her husband, it is possible for a female to alter her status through marriage.[7] Also, since the specific ranking and status systems vary somewhat from community to community, it is possible to alter status through physical mobility.

Finally, it should be noted that the greater the degree of vertical mobility associated with any stratification system, the more diffuse are the class boundaries of that system. In a mobile class system, boundaries between classes can only be arbitrarily determined. At the same time, the differential effects of *relative* status

[6] John W. Bennett, and Melvin Tumin, *Social Life* (New York: Alfred A. Knopf, 1948), pp. 46ff.

[7] Harry C. Bredemeier, and Richard M. Stephenson, *The Analyses of Social Systems* (New York: Holt, Rinehart and Winston, 1962), pp. 322–333.

assignment may be noted in terms of such things as material rewards, prestige, and behavior patterns of varying types.

Some Approaches to the Identification of Social Classes and Social Mobility In view of the assumed diffuseness of class boundaries and the need for some more or less arbitrary but meaningful measure of social class and social mobility, brief attention is given here to some of the more prominent approaches that have been utilized by researchers.

The more generally accepted measures of social class might be grouped in terms of three major types. One of these might be referred to as the *objective, multiple-factor, index* type. The Index of Status Characteristics, devised by W. Lloyd Warner, is probably one of the best examples of this type of measure of social class.[8] Briefly, this approach results in the assignment of the individual to a status level, based upon weighted values that are attached to the individual's occupation, source of income, type of house, and type of dwelling area.

A second general type of measure might be referred to as the *objective, single-factor* type. Basically, this involves the utilization of one of the rank systems in the society. Attention is focused on the rank system that appears to be one of the most important in the social system. While both income category and educational achievement level have been used separately for such purposes, the most common rank system utilized has been that of occupational position. In their respective studies, Richard Centers[9] and C. Wright Mills[10] have relied upon the occupational factor as their measure of social class.

It is necessary to have some familiarity with the relative positions in the ranking system of occupation to use this single factor effectively. Considerable insight into this field of knowledge was provided through a nationwide study of occupational prestige by

[8] W. Lloyd Warner, M. Meeker, and K. Eells, *Social Class in America* (Chicago: Science Research Associates, 1949).

[9] Richard Centers, *The Psychology of Social Classes* (Princeton, N. J.: Princeton University Press, 1949).

[10] C. Wright Mills, "Middle Classes in Middle Sized Cities," *American Sociological Review,* II (December, 1949), pp. 220–229.

the National Opinion Research Center.[11] In this study a representative sample of adult Americans was asked to rate nearly one hundred occupations in terms of what the respondents considered to be their desirability. The resulting scale of occupational prestige has been helpful in assigning individuals to appropriate class levels.

The third type of measure of social class might be referred to as the *subjective, evaluation* approach. This approach is predicated on the assumption that each individual has some general consciousness of his or her class position and that this information may be secured simply by asking the person for it. One of the most notable uses of this approach was that of Richard Centers in his widely known study.[12] Centers found that while there was a significant correlation between the class assignment based on a subjective evaluation and that based on occupation, there was some tendency for the former measure to result in a more frequent assignment to a middle class position.

Since a measure of social mobility represents measurements of social class position for at least two different times in the life of an individual, one would expect the measures of social mobility to be the same as those of social class. Taking account of problems of such things as the availability of data and the validity of data, there has been some tendency to emphasize occupational changes as the measuring stick of social mobility. Lipset and Bendix used this criterion.[13] Social mobility is also indicated across generations when children acquire occupational statuses that are higher or lower than the occupational statuses of their fathers. Natalie Rogoff, for example, obtained such information from marriage license applications on which the applicants had given their occupations and the occupations of their fathers.[14]

[11] "Jobs and Occupations: A Popular Evaluation," *Opinion News,* IV (September, 1947), pp. 3–13.

[12] Centers, *op. cit.*

[13] Seymour Martin Lipset, and Reinhard Bendix, *Social Mobility in Industrial Society* (Berkeley: University of California Press, 1960), p. 6.

[14] Natalie Rogoff, "Recent Trends in Occupational Mobility," in *Class, Status and Power,* eds. Reinhard Bendix, and Seymour Martin Lipset (Glencoe, Ill.: The Free Press, 1963), pp. 442–453.

Once stratification systems are identified (usually on a community level) and once the criteria are employed in identification of the class memberships of individuals, class-based behaviors can be discerned. Some differences are explainable on obvious grounds. Individuals with more income are naturally going to exhibit different consumer patterns. Social contacts are going to be limited or increased by one's economic resources. Other class-based differences are not as obvious or expected. Differential behavior patterns of individuals from various parts of the class structure include some interesting variations.[15]

1. Infant mortality rate decreases as socioeconomic status increases.
2. Middle and upper class persons have a longer life expectancy than working class persons.
3. Birth rates decrease with higher class position.
4. Age of marriage increases with rises in class level.
5. Working class males begin heterosexual activity earlier and have more frequent sex activity than do middle and upper class males.
6. Divorce rates decrease as status level rises except for "the new upper class," the "jet set," and "cafe society."
7. Working class persons focus their social life more around the home, family, and relatives than do middle class people.
8. Membership in organizations increases as status increases.
9. Child rearing practices vary by class. The indications are that lower status parents tend to be more permissive in child raising (especially toilet training) than are middle class parents.
10. Children from lower status homes are less likely to finish high school and are less likely to get college preparatory education (recent changes are in progress, however).

[15] See Ely Chinoy, *Society: An Introduction to Sociology* (New York: Random, 1962) pp. 154–157; use of p. 155 granted by University of Chicago Press. See also, Alvin Gouldner, and Helen Gouldner, *Modern Sociology* (Harcourt Brace Jovanovich, 1963), pp. 237–244.

11. Illnesses with longer disabling effects are more frequent among the lower class than those above them.

12. Wartime casualty rates for males are directly related to status and racial determinants. Casualty rates become lower as income level rises.

Also introduced earlier was the concept of mobility, or movement through the class structure. Some interesting observations have been made regarding the differences between those individuals who are upwardly mobile and those who are not.[16]

1. Loss of status by a spouse produces an unstable marriage.

2. Upwardly mobile spouses make poor adjustments after marriage.

3. Effects of upward mobility on children include feelings of insecurity and isolation.

4. Upwardly mobile individuals reject norms of the stratum they are leaving and seek to incorporate those of the stratum they are striving for, i.e., political attitudes, prejudices, etc.

What are the cultural norms and traits that the socially mobile either reject or seek to incorporate? Or, more generally, are there class-based subcultures, and if so, how do they characterize a class?

These questions are answered to some degree in the research of August B. Hollingshead.[17] Hollingshead christened the community he studied as Elmtown. Having once established the class structure of this community and identified his subjects (535 families) as to their membership in the classes, his continuing observations revealed, "The possession of a constellation of differentially evaluated social symbols—functional, pecuniary, religious, educational, reputational, power lineage, proper associates, memberships in associations—are relied upon by Elmtowners to 'hang

[16] "Consequences of Social Mobility in the United States," *Transactions of the Third World Congress of Sociology* (London: International Sociological Association, 1956), III, p. 195.

[17] August B. Hollingshead, *Elmtown's Youth: The Impact of Social Classes on Adolescents* (New York: John Wiley, 1949), pp. 83–120. By permission of John Wiley & Sons, Inc.

people on the peg they belong on. . . .' "[18] Hollingshead found the classes to be differentiated in a number of ways.

Class I   The Upper Class

1. Membership is stabilized from generation to generation by wealth and lineage combined through economic, legal, and family systems.

2. Position in this class is seldom achieved, but rather ascribed by inheritance.

3. Marriage between social equals is desired and achieved in four out of five cases. Threat of a marriage to one of a lower stratum brings strong social pressure to break off the affair.

4. Children are born in a large city hospital, carefully attended and well educated.

5. The men are engaged in business or forming enterprises and have the highest incomes in the community.

6. Understandably, this group has an interest in keeping tax and assessment rates low, which they accomplish through the control of the two major party organizations.

7. All homes are owned. Consumption does not exhaust income. Therefore, a sizeable portion of their income is saved or reinvested.

8. Most families have three cars—paid for—the business car, the family car, and a car for the young folks.

9. Leisure, not labor, is dignified. One spends as little time as is necessary in making a living. Hunting and fishing provide leisure for men, various clubs provide leisure for women, and the country club fills in what time is left.

Class II   The Upper Middle Class

1. Prestige is related as much to civic leadership as to economics.

---

[18] *Ibid.*

2. These are the "outwardly prominent prestige bearers of the community." Often, however, they are controlled from behind the scenes by powerful Class I families.

3. Most of these families trace their ancestry to "pioneer American stock." The rest are third generation German, Norwegian, or Irish.

4. Most live in the "best" residential sections, owning their own nicely furnished homes. Older "charming" homes are the most prized, as some were once inhabited by Class I families.

5. Income comes from the practice of a profession by the male in the family (law, medicine, engineering, and dentistry). Some have a family-owned business or are salaried executives in Class I enterprises.

6. Most income is spent on family living and only a fraction is left for saving and investment. "Prudence in spending is exercised widely."

7. Wives are homemakers, mothers, and social secretaries with the help of a part-time general domestic servant. Also they are expected to be involved in women's community activities.

8. Parents share the responsibility of rearing the children, making sacrifices to give them advantages. Boys are steered to business or a profession, girls are prepared for a desirable marriage.

9. Every family is affiliated with, or active in, church work, predominantly Protestant.

10. Leisure time is limited and money for extensive travel is limited. They spend some time at the country club for "golf and gossip."

Class III   The Lower Middle Class

1. The greater portion of this group derives their livelihood from wages and salaries, the remainder own small businesses, farms, or practice a profession.

2. This group reveals strong class feelings, or class consciousness, knowing full well the superiority of Classes I and II regarding wealth, leisure, way of life, leadership, and social activity.

3. A small portion of mothers in this class work to supplement family income. They are generally teachers, nurses, and stenographers who received their training prior to marriage. Some of these working mothers are supporting a family after a husband's death.

4. This group has sufficient income for living but scarce surplus for investment. Most income is spent on consumer goods. Quantity of things is stressed rather than quality.

5. They live primarily in second best or old residential areas. About two-thirds own their own homes.

6. They are active in church work. Sunday schools are staffed mainly by these people.

7. They are not as well educated as Class II people. Most have completed high school, but only a few are trained beyond that. Wives are generally better educated than their husbands.

8. Leisure is spent in sex- and age-segregated lodges, patriotic clubs, etc. Very few acquire coveted membership in the country club or Rotary.

9. Class III people are very active politically, but not powerful.

10. A few names from this class show up in police records. No names are from Class I or II. Either they are more likely to commit an offense or they lack power to avoid formal charges following an offense.

Class IV   The Upper Lower Class

1. The members of Class IV are wage earners working in the mines, mills, and shops of Elmtown. About one-third of the mothers work to supplement income.

2. Income is large enough to provide the necessities but

few comforts or luxuries. Income is spent as earned, very little being left over for a "rainy day."

3. Meager life savings are spent in buying a small home on contract or through a mortgage to a local bank. Only one-third own, or are buying, their own home.

4. Only a small portion have savings, commercial bank accounts, or bank credit.

5. The family stability of the other three classes gives way to instability in this class. They marry early, start families earlier, and have more children.

6. Most of the wife's time is spent on family duties; there is no hired help and membership in women's clubs is rare.

7. Educational experience is limited. When this study was made (1942), Hollingshead found only a few who had completed high school.

8. This class is not active in religious activity. When the women are active, they are found in the kitchen at a church dinner.

9. Civic and community organizations are outside of the experience of these people. The organizations they are active in are usually local unions. Leisure activities are rare.

10. Convictions for crime are higher among this class than among Class III.

Class V   The Lower Lower Class

1. Income comes from a variety of sources in this class. Fathers are the chief breadwinners in three-fourths of the families. Over half of the wives work out of the home. Earnings are meager for both, who work primarily in unskilled jobs.

2. Uncertain nature of employment results in long periods of idleness for this class. Illness also results in layoffs. Employers hire them only when labor is scarce or when they can be induced to work for low wages.

3. Many of these families have lived in Elmtown as long as the leading families—since before the Civil War. Unfor-

tunately, the unsavory reputations of ancestors are re-membered.

4. They live in dilapidated box-like homes containing worn furniture. A wood or coal stove is used for both heating and cooking.

5. Privacy in the home is almost nonexistent. All living is done in two or three rooms.

6. The family is rather unstable—desertion, divorce, and death are frequent. Sexual liaisons between higher class males and Class V teenage girls occur, but rarely does marriage follow.

7. Formal education is limited mainly to elementary school.

8. Leisure time is spent in informal visits between neighbors or just "loafing" around. Very few people gain or seek membership in organizations. The major social activity is Saturday night at the tavern.

9. These families are better known by the police, the sheriff, and the prosecuting attorney than by ministers or school officials.

10. Almost half of the males have been convicted of a crime.

Admittedly Hollingshead's study was done in 1942. Changes have occurred. However, the changes are relative to all classes. Research done by this author in 1961 in a small Missouri Valley town, comparable in size to Elmtown, revealed the same pat-terns.[19]

Classes are real, people are ranked, people know their relative rank position. Beyond that the class phenomenon is much more complex than those stated by Marx. There are more subtle motiva-tions at work than pure economics. However, the economic situa-tion is the base upon which these determinants work. We are as yet only beginning to understand the interplay of these complex variables.

---

[19] Alan F. Jensen, *Stratification in a Prairie Town.* Unpublished Master's thesis, University of South Dakota, Vermillion, 1961.

Chapter 7   The Nature of Religion in Human Societies

It is said that roughly one-fifteenth of the books published every year in the United States are in the area of religion. This means about 2,000 titles each year. A good third of these are specifically of a denominational nature (hymnbooks, catechisms, etc.). Of the remainder, there are probably 200 serious titles that "shape the course of religion."[1]

Of these 200 serious titles, it is likely that only a handful are of a sociological nature, i.e., books which seek to describe and analyze the impact of religion on society and vice versa, or books which seek to analyze the "functional" aspects of the religious structure. One might take this as an indicator of just how rare the serious, abstract, and analytic discussions of religion are. Most individuals have, it would appear, some particularized vested in-

[1] *Newsweek,* March 29, 1969, p. 90.

terest in their own denominational memberships and theologies. No doubt many people feel that either heaven or their social position might be jeopardized if they were to verbalize an objective analysis of this phenomenon called religion. However, as has been indicated earlier, the sociologist wants to know and he wants to know exactly. What follows, then, is a summary of a variety of these analyses.

This chapter will present the various ways in which religion, especially of the western cultures, is analyzed by sociologists and sociologically oriented theologians. There are at least four distinct approaches to the nature of religion which are not assumed by the author to be an exhaustive list, but will, it is hoped, give the reader a perspective on the sociology of religion.

1. The anthropological-functional approach (macro-sociological) of Max Weber.
2. The sociological-functional approach of Milton Yinger (bordering on the level of micro-sociology).
3. The ethics approach of Reinhold Niebuhr.
4. The existential and personalistic approach of Martin Buber.

THE ANTHROPOLOGICAL-FUNCTIONAL APPROACH OF MAX WEBER[2] The author has referred to Max Weber's analysis as being functional. You are wondering, no doubt, what this means. As a mode of analysis functionalism has certain distinguishing features. It is a way of looking at society in which society is perceived as a system or an organic whole, the various parts of which are all integrated into an ongoing enterprise. As such, it is an attempt to:

1. Indicate the self-maintaining system and its boundaries.
2. Observe what's happening at all levels in such a system in order to establish:
   a. The purpose which each part of the system accomplishes for the whole.
   b. The relationship between each part of the system.

---

[2] Max Weber, *Sociology of Religion,* trans. Ephraim Fischoff (Boston: Beacon Press, 1963).

3. Observe how certain characteristics peculiar to the system are maintained after having identified the existence of each characteristic.

4. Observe the interplay of each of the parts over time to get an indication of change in the system.[3]

Max Weber's approach to religion is functional because Weber notes the various substructures or parts in the larger system or society, noting how each influences the others, how the larger system is maintained, how change comes about in one part, how this influences the other parts, and how society is then an ongoing, dynamic, complex process.

Taking religion as the point of reference, Weber notes how it is elaborately intertwined with the structures of law, economics, social class, the family, the intellectuals. Weber further indicates how subtle change within one part is related to changes in general in the ongoing society. He includes in his account both eastern and western religions. For our purpose, let us look at his analysis of the Judeo-Christian influence in the western world.

> Religiously motivated behavior is relatively rational behavior, especially in its earliest manifestations. It follows rules of experience . . . . Rubbing will elicit sparks from pieces of wood, and, in like fashion, the stimulative actions of a magician will evoke rain from the heavens.[4]

Thus begins Weber's treatise. He makes it a point to emphasize that religious behavior in its beginnings is oriented to practical "this world" problems. Man finds himself in an environment that is hostile but evidently manipulatable. At least, those forces which control existence may be appealed to and appeased. Certain individuals who display an ability to deal with these forces and sway them for the group's benefit are said to be endowed with "charisma" and take on roles of religious leadership. Ostensibly, this charisma is an ability to hypnotize (so to speak) collectives of

---

[3] Richard H. Ogles, from a lecture delivered at Washington State University, Pullman, 1963.

[4] Weber, *op. cit.,* p. 1.

humans. Over time the quasi-scientific magician is replaced by the prophet—an emissary from the greater force. The prophet establishes a religious community from those to whom his charisma is appealing. Later, in a rational and businesslike way a priest arises who has the role of executing the ritual and maintaining the everyday existence of the religious establishment. Over time ritual evolves into law. As with the pre-Christian Roman religion, correct religious behavior was also proper etiquette and good citizenship.

In both primitive and modern thought, abstractions are employed. Manipulating and manipulated force in the environment becomes abstracted to "spirit" and "anima," and notions of the "other world" arise. From the basic dualisms of "spirit-substance" and "this world-other world," more elaborate dualisms arise. A list of these would include "good-evil," "heaven-hell," and "body-soul." Notions of a continued life in this "other world" ensue, followed by concomitant notions of salvation and damnation. The charismatic leaders who, by use of alcohol, incense, drugs, or sexual orgasm, experience ecstasy by claiming to have glimpses of this "other world." Hence, the keys to this ecstasy are usually controlled and their use is limited by the magician-priest. This may be a fairly plausible explanation for societal taboos regarding tobacco, alcohol, and prostitution in primitive societies, many of which are still with us today. In most societies, sex and intoxication are ritualized. As the religious establishment evolves, such orgiastic behavior, which has been promoted by the magician, is denounced by the prophet, and then replaced by less expressive behavior by the priest, who makes ecstasy more routine and brings it into the intellectual realm. Likewise the spirit world becomes more and more abstracted until most of the other world is symbolized by a single, personalized figure, "The great I AM," or "God," or "King of Kings." This process is never complete, however. As with Christianity there still exists a whole hierarchy of lesser gods and anti-gods. Along with this evolution, the manifest function of religion shifts from manipulation of the hostile environment to a search for a meaning for existence. And, if there exist inconsistencies in the social-economic system, religions offer salvation and an ultimate goal of eternal bliss as the meaning of life.

As societies become more complex and there is a social differentiation to the extent that great divergencies exist in privileges and availability of goods, religion functions as a cohesive agent rationalizing the advantages of the privileged class and offering ultimate reward to those less fortunate. If it fails to do this, the cynicism of the not-so-privileged manifests itself in a new prophet and the establishment of a counter-religion. Weber notes this general development in the Judeo-Christian tradition, specifying that the later forms of religious establishment are intellectual endeavors. Such was the Judaism of the first century B.C. and Christianity since St. Thomas Acquinas.

According to Weber, religion functions as the focal point of social change. Sometimes it is a conservative barrier to change, sometimes a stabilizer for a society undergoing rapid change, and sometimes a planter of the seeds of change. The role that religion plays in change in any particular situation depends on certain social characteristics of the believers. These characteristics are referred to by Weber as Asceticism and Mysticism. Asceticism involves a dissatisfaction with the social structure coupled with a realization that religion is a part of that structure and a belief that salvation comes through a rational endeavor to change these situations. Mysticism, on the other hand, is a renunciation of this world and of sensual contact with it. It is basically a self-centered approach to a world that never seems to approach utopia. The religions which have been most functional have been those marked by a preponderance of asceticism. Christianity, in its history, has been marked by several periods of both mysticism and asceticism, whereas Judaism since the first century A.D. has been characterized by a this-worldly approach. Many historians see the asceticism of Judaism as the prime mover in western man's scientific evolution.

THE SOCIOLOGICAL-FUNCTIONAL APPROACH OF MILTON YINGER   Yinger's work represents not only an analysis but also an assessment of the relative ability of religion to function in the modern complex and urban society of the twentieth century.[5]

---

[5] Milton Yinger, *Religion, Society and the Individual* (New York: Macmillan, 1957).

Yinger profiles the conditions of twentieth century America while depicting the institution of religion within it. He then indicates some fruitful areas of research in the area of religion. In brief review, how does religion function in our society? Yinger indicates some observations which might appear to be paradoxical.

First, there is an increase in secularism (nonsacred) combined with an increase in church memberships and religious consciousness (sacred). Second, there is an increasing heterogeneity of faith (differentness) coupled with an increase in the homogeneity of American values (sameness). Under closer scrutiny these are not such paradoxical observations. Yinger maintains that the increase in religious consciousness is also secular (asceticism). The urban church and the young minister and priest have developed very this-worldly attitudes. He believes that the religious establishment is becoming keenly aware of social problems and therefore it is a movement very much akin to other secular movements in society.

The second paradox disappears when it is suggested that the outward conformity which gives the appearance of a homogeneous culture is really a reaction to heterogeneous values. It is in his religion alone that man can express his cynicism of broader cultural values even though daily life demands conformity to them. In this sense the most functional religion is the cult-like or pentecostal type which acts as a buffer for those non-privileged or alienated members of society. They also serve as a check on the highly structured religious groups that traditionally function as a conservative force maintaining, "Let every soul be subject to the powers that be, for the powers that be are ordained by God." Says Yinger:

> Once again I must remark that those who define religion solely in terms of individual salvation are likely to dismiss this as an irrelevant statement. Economic and political questions are no concern of religion, they will argue; the growth of slums at the heart of our metropolitan areas is doubtless an unhappy event, but this has no bearing on the problem of man's salvation. For my part, I doubt if one can separate the functions in this way. In search for some ultimate meaning to exis-

tence, some system of belief that lends dignity to life and makes its suffering less poignant, few men are likely to be persuaded by a religion that disregards the conflicts and institutions that make life harsh and meaningless for many.[6]

THE ETHICS APPROACH OF REINHOLD NIEBUHR *Moral Man and Immoral Society* represents a conflict orientation of a conception of society, with the religious institution as the focus of concern.[7] Rather than dialectic materialism, it might be referred to as dialectic nonmaterialism, i.e., having reference to class struggle which is based not only on economics, but on spiritual values as well. The implication here is rather vague, so, to put it bluntly, the book is a well-written indictment against the industrial and military elites of the 1930s.

The core of the argument is this: the collective (society) is a magnification of all the vices and egoisms of the individuals involved. It is impossible to right social wrongs at the conference table because individuals themselves behave morally only in the face of coercion. The same is true with collectives of individuals. An industrial elite in America does not pay income tax and good wages because this is the good and moral thing to do. It is done because the workers as a counter-collective have matched their will and power and have used coercion. Is it then the destiny of man to live in a society which is moral only to the extent that it is coerced? What resources for moral behavior does man have at his disposal save force as a power balance? First, man has rational resources. But, it has been demonstrated through history that an increase in societal cohesion and moral behavior does not appreciably erase ignorance. The primitive can act out of sympathy if he wants to, and the educated man can shoot striking workers. Surely, increased rationalism would be an aid in the development of the good society, but more is needed.

What about religious resources?

---

[6] *Ibid.,* p. 26.

[7] Reinhold Niebuhr, *Moral Man and Immoral Society* (New York: Charles Scribner's Sons, 1932).

If the recognition of selfishness is prerequisite to the mitigation of its force and the diminution of its anti-social consequences in society, religion should be a dominant influence in the socialization (moral attainment) of man; for religion is fruitful of the spirit of contrition. Feeling himself under the scrutiny of an omniscient eye, and setting his puny will into juxtaposition with an holy and omnipotent will, the religious man is filled with a sense of shame for the impertinence of his self-centered life.[8]

But, again, moral attitudes develop most sensitively in person-to-person relationships and apply only in those situations or ones like them. Abstracted morals do not have the hold on man that personalized morals do. Hence, the privileged classes become hypocritical and seek to enhance their prestige at the cost of the underprivileged, rationalized by the religious establishment. This in turn brings about a cynicism of the underprivileged with regard to a religion that offers them only a deferred reward.

What is the answer? It is necessary for each individual to feel morally responsible for an evil society and to act for a dissolution of this evil. How? By coercion. By a steady and sure application of nonviolent force upon those elements which are inconsistent with humane society. This, too, is a kind of religion. "Religion is the magnification of all that is good in man."

THE EXISTENTIAL-PERSONALISTIC APPROACH OF MARTIN BUBER This approach also focuses on the predicament of man in a modern, complex society. F. H. Heinemann, in *Existentialism and the Modern Predicament,* indicates that the existentialist may be the spiritual leader of our time.[9]

Why? Because he speaks of the predicament of man in a machine age—an age which has resulted in the agglomeration and collectivization of millions of people in great cities and has

---

[8] *Ibid.,* p. 51.

[9] F. H. Heinemann, *Existentialism and the Modern Predicament* (New York: Harper and Row, 1958).

brought about the depersonalization of man—the total breakup and rupture of human relations between men and between men and the natural world. Even the artist, says Heinemann, falls prey to using techniques which result in his alienation from his creativity. If there is a common denominator by which to identify existential thought, it is in opposition to contemporary systems of thought which treat the world with naturalistic mechanisms of logic and technique and transform everything into an object of calculation and control—man included. Existentialists call for a return to concrete experience and reality, including the reality of man discovering himself as a free agent who can challenge a world that supresses him—an awakening of man to the fact that he is a spiritual being endeavoring to be extraordinary.

One representative of this orientation is Martin Buber.[10] Rather than a sociology of religion, Buber's writings in this area represent a theology of society. It is an attempt at an objective analysis of our times and man's spiritual needs.

Buber begins by noting that neither the single individual nor the social aggregate is the fundamental fact of human existence. The fundamental fact is man with man. That unique thing (the self) which is characteristic of all that is human is that which takes place between one person and another (interaction). The essence of human life is what happens between man and man and between man and himself. This continued dialogue is *soul* or *spirit*. But, there is another dimension, namely, man interacting with God. The dialogue is of two kinds—the I-It dialogue and the I-Thou dialogue, each of which is characteristic of an attitude toward life.

The I-It relationship is that of the self relating to the world as a collective of objects which the self uses for its purposes, primarily for the purpose of orientation. One finds his locus—his direction—in the matrix. But this is an artificial relation to the world. It is secure and anchored but it leaves the I essentially alone, bouncing among the Its.

The second type of dialogue with the world is the I-Thou rela-

[10] From an interpretation of Buber's work. See Paul Pfuetze, *Self, Society and Existence* (New York: Harper and Row, 1961).

tionship. This is a cognizance of the other selves, other souls, other Is, and the attitude is one of actualizing—finding the ultimate reality, although a reality which is not empirically verifiable as was the It. The I-Thou relation is pure relation with the other—knowing the other and letting oneself be known. Buber believes that the crucial importance of such relations between people is the redeeming message for our dehumanized world. The I-Thou relation between individuals and the natural world is also important. Says Buber, it is usually found only among primitives and children. To the child a tree is not an It, it is a Thou. Buber hypothesizes that the first thought of a child is Thou, an exclamation of relatedness with the world that surrounds him, another self. It is in this I-Thou relationship that man may eventually experience community rather than just mere organization or association. Buber realizes that man cannot survive totally in only one of the two worlds of relations; he believes that man's survival on this planet necessitates an increase in the I-Thou dialogue.

Religion is then the dialogic life in history—the summons to man and his response. The Bible is the age-old record of this dialogue between God and man—address and answer—revelation and response.

> Man is called by the world and by his fellowmen and he must give answer. Nature, beauty, neighbor, God— everything speaks to him, crying for release, for the right word. God speaks and the world answers, the world is created. God speaks and man answers and he becomes a person, a self.[11]

Pfuetze sums it up well by indicating that Mead and Buber, in developing doctrines of the social self, have succeeded in formulating a theory and a strategy which can better harmonize the individual with the social good, liberty with order, freedom with necessity, mechanism with teleology, and God with man.[12]

---

[11] *Ibid.,* p. 129.
[12] *Ibid.,* pp. 229–288.

SUMMARY

In reviewing these four approaches to the nature of religion, the author has sought to indicate two general aspects of the sociology of religion. First, the sociology of religion is an objective analysis of the structuring and functioning of a social institution, and second, it is an analysis of the predicament of man and concomitantly a philosophy of action to lift man out of this predicament. Surely it cannot be both at the same time. Milton Yinger has indicated that complete objectivity would lack the basic interest and the sympathy necessary for the development of a religious appeal. On the other hand, too great an investment in the religious establishment would mean that all objectivity would be lost. In order for the sociology of religion to progress, it must have research and analysis accomplished by men who see purpose or who can at least posit purpose to the ongoing evolutionary struggle of the creature called man.

Chapter 8   Bureaucracy and Complex Organizations

Modern man is man in organizations. If the most dramatic fact that sets our stage apart from earlier ones is that we live today under the shadow of nuclear destruction, the most pervasive feature that distinguishes contemporary life is that it is dominated by large, complex, and formal organizations. Our ability to organize thousands and even millions of men in order to accomplish large scale tasks—be they economic, political, or military—is one of our greatest strengths. The possibility that free men become mere cogs in the bureaucratic machineries set up for this purpose is one of the greatest threats to our liberty.[1]

[1] Peter M. Blau, and Richard Scott, *Formal Organizations* (San Francisco: Chandler Press, 1962), Chapter IX.

The term bureaucracy has become one of those overused and, hence, almost unintelligible terms in our language. Some people use the term as an adjective to evaluate negatively the disturbing aspects of organizational life, as the red tape, ritualism, inefficiency, and "go slowism" of organizations that we commonly come in contact with. Others use it as a verb which translated means "to gum up the works" or "to divide and conquer." To others, it is a noun which is synonymous with security and fringe benefits. To the sociologist, it is all of these and none of these. It is a term which denotes a certain form of activity and interaction in which human beings sometimes are involved. It is a form of group organization which is marked by those secondary relations we talked about in an earlier chapter and it is so structured intentionally. Ideally, the intentional patterning of human interaction to insure impartiality, impersonal relations, specialization, and simplicity is done in order to increase the efficiency of the combined efforts of many individuals in attaining some specified goal.

In reality, however, such an ideal is sought with varied success. Goals are not always shared by all members of the organization. Sometimes efficiency becomes an end in itself rather than a means to an end. Sometimes organizational life itself becomes the end for many individuals who grow to depend upon the organizational blanket that is their security. Sometimes, organizational life means nothing more to many of its members than the correct repetition of ritual behaviors for a specified amount of time at the end of which is a gold watch and a monthly retirement check, not to mention the benefits of the group burial insurance. Whatever it is, it is the form of social organization that characterizes the work situation of the majority of individuals in western culture. Thus, it is to our best advantage to understand as well as we can.

CHARACTERISTICS OF THE IDEAL BUREAUCRACY The following characterization of modern bureaucracy is an interpretation and paraphrasing of the work of Max Weber from a translation by A. M. Henderson and Talcott Parsons.[2] It is a description of the

[2] Max Weber, *The Theory of Social and Economic Organization,* trans. A. M. Henderson, and Talcott Parsons (New York: Oxford University Press, 1947), pp. 329–340.

ideal bureaucracy, a sum total of traits from all individual bureaucracies, a pure form which, in all probability, never really exists in any actual bureaucratic organization.

The major definitive characteristics of bureaucratic organization in western culture of the nineteenth and twentieth centuries are rationalization and legalism. These characteristics are distinctly modern patterns and represent the break with preindustrial patterns of spontaneity and charismatic authority.

Spontaneity refers to a process of group organization in which the organization of individuals and their efforts occurs by trial and error processes. Statuses and roles emerge as their need arises and sometimes persist for some time after their need disappears. Members of the organization see the emerging order as being ordained by the supernatural in that they cannot perceive any human intentions behind the development of the order. An example would be the preindustrial feudal order of Europe. This order had a great hold over the masses of unsophisticated people because to deviate was not to break an organizational rule, but rather to sin against God. Logically enough, the authority patterns were based on charismatic authority, as in the "divine right of kings" or as in the pronouncements of infallibility by leaders of the religious establishment.

On the other hand, bureaucratic organization in its pure form is the product of rational construction. It is an engineered organization of individuals, designed and constructed for a particular purpose. Theoretically, the control of its members is through rules, codes, statutes; that is, a constitution that is arrived at democratically. The authority structure is that which is referred to as legal authority—leadership by consensus of the led. Moreover, the authority structure is not a single office of a king (or something similar), but a number of offices, each one having a specified jurisdiction in organizational life. Weber has indicated that the effectiveness of this legal authority rests upon acceptance of the validity of certain ideas which the author has paraphrased below.

The rules, or legal norms, are established either by agreement or by imposition, but to be able to enjoy obedience they must be established on grounds of expediency (usually called "operating procedures") and/or rational values. These rules are linked in a consistent body of law, that is, they do not contradict each other.

The administration of the organization is the pursuit of organizational goals within the limits of these rules. This is true also for each individual who administers his office in the organization. Each member obeys this law. He owes no obedience to any other member or person in authority, but only to the impersonal order of the organization. His superiors may not make personal claims on him, only legal claims.

The fundamental aspects of rational-legal authority are the following. There is an ongoing organization of official actions bound by the rules of the organization. There is a specific sphere of competence or organizational territory for each status in the organization. The sphere of competence or territory over which an individual has jurisdiction, by virtue of the office he occupies, includes obligations to perform certain actions, the authority to do this, and the necessary means to insure cooperation from other offices in the completion of these official actions.

All of the offices or statuses are organized upon the principle of hierarchy. Each lower office is under the jurisdiction and supervision of a higher one. Likewise, each lower office has the right of appeal to the higher office if it has a grievance, as in a case where a higher office pursues a course of action which is not legal or is outside of its jurisdiction.

Only a person who has demonstrated adequate training to allow official duties to be carried out correctly in the specific office for which he is applying may occupy that office. Should he wish to compete for an appointment to a higher office in the hierarchy, he must have the talents, training, and ability to carry out the functions in that sphere of activity.

All activity of the organization such as administrative acts, decisions, and rules are formulated and recorded in writing. The combinations of written documents and the ongoing official functions constitute the bureau or the office.

The administrative staff arranged in hierarchy under the supreme authority consists of individual officials who are appointed and function according to the following criteria:

1. In their private lives they are free, being subject to authority only with respect to their impersonal official obligations. They are subject to the legal demands of their

superior only during office hours, or when they are acting for the organization.

2. All officials are related to each other in a hierarchy of offices. The relationships are those of superiors and subordinates.

3. Each of these offices represents a specific territory of jurisdiction for which the officeholder has demonstrated competence. This is established legally by rules spelled out in the constitution.

4. Each office is filled by a free contractual agreement between the incumbent and the organization.

5. Candidates compete for selection as officeholders and are selected on the basis of their qualifications. Usually this is established by examinations or guaranteed by diplomas issued by the school which trained the candidate.

6. For carrying out his official duties as legally established, the officeholder is remunerated by a legally established fixed salary and usually there is a pension at the time of retirement. Only under specified conditions may the employing authority terminate the individual's employment. However, the official is always free to resign. The salary is established on the basis of the rank of the official, the nature of his responsibilities, and the requirements of his social status.

7. The office is regarded as the only occupation or at least the principal occupation of the officeholder.

8. The office of the incumbent is his career. There is usually a system of promotion to a higher rank in the hierarchy or increased salary based on seniority and/or achievement and this is decided by one's superiors.

9. The official works separately from the ownership of the means of administration.

10. The official is subject to strict and systematic discipline and control when conducting his official functions.

The above are the essential items in a description of an ideal bureaucratic structure. Theoretically, when these criteria are met, the organization accomplishes a task expediently and economically. But what actually happens when human beings are plugged into offices and the bureaucracy goes into action? Does it work? Sometimes it works surprisingly well. At other times the attempt is less successful.

FORMAL ORGANIZATIONS—LIVING WITH REALITIES As was indicated earlier, Weber's characterization represents the ideal, a measuring stick by which we can judge the relative bureaucratization of any given formal organization. If it is observed, for instance, that a particular organization does not accomplish its organizational goals efficiently, we can hardly say, "Yeh, that's bureaucracy for you"; rather, we should make the judgment that the organization in question is really falling short of being a bureaucracy. This is to say that the assumptions of the rational-legal authority structure have not been met, or that the criteria of official function and expertise are not being followed.

Obviously, the various so-called bureaucracies with which the average American deals daily reveal varied success in administrative efficiency. Almost everyone has a favorite story to tell about some mix-up in their dealings with an organization—a one cent tax return sent by certified check, a draft notice and discharge papers sent on the same day, a letter received in 1969 that was mailed in 1928, approval of credit on the same day that the bank forecloses. These are all interesting little items for after-dinner conversation. But they are interesting precisely because they are rare. The real problems of bureaucracy are seldom immediately observable and have long-range effects on society as a whole. Over and above the notion of problems incurred when organizations do not meet the ideal, there are even suggestions that in the ideal state bureaucracies may have long-range problematic effects. Max Weber indicated some of the more general consequences of bureaucratic control as populations tend increasingly to be organized in these large-scale corporate groups.

Weber's list of social consequences includes the following, which we shall discuss before going on to contemporary research in the analysis of formal organizations.

1. The consequence of leveling and centralization.
2. The consequence of permanence.
3. The consequence of rationalization of education.

Leveling and Centralization   Leveling is a term that refers to the disappearance of certain social and economic differences among the members of an organization or a society—a disappearance of clear distinctions between statuses or between individuals. It is the social extension of the nonpolitical dimensions of democratization. The political definitions of democracy usually are references to the self-government of homogeneous units of men granted to them by the larger super-unit, i.e., the granting of freedom by a colonial power to a new nation, or as in states' rights, or as the rights of smaller units in society to have involvement in decision making by acquiring representation in the legislative processes of the super-unit. Weber indicates that this political democratization is a precondition for the rise of bureaucracies in western societies, i.e., "the abstract regularity of the execution of authority" which requires consensus regarding the law.

On the other hand, leveling (social democracy) may be seen logically as a consequence of the bureaucratization of society and probably is the same phenomenon that is referred to by other analysts of society as "mass society." It eventually results in a break with "traditional rule by notables which is based upon personal relationships and personal esteem." The shift in bureaucracy from notables (both the elected and inherited varieties) to tenured officials results in the "leveling of the governed" under impersonal universal rules (no special cases), the "highly articulated group of officials may then occupy quite an autocratic position although their authority is within constitutionally established boundaries." It is interesting to note here that current social-political movements for change are, it would seem, reactions to the power of appointed officials. This is a much different thing from the movements of the nineteenth century which were reactions against monarchies.

This problem of leveling becomes amplified as bureaucracies grow larger and more encompassing, resulting in the increased centralization of official functions and decision making. For instance, in the California state college system, all of the campuses are essentially governed by a board of appointed officials (trustees) rather than each campus governing itself. This is done in the name of efficiency, utilizing impersonal execution of authority and universal formulae; however, as Weber predicted, it results in a leveling of the governed and an actual increase in cash outlay because the ratio of paid administrative officials increases rather than decreases.

This brings up the next problem.

Permanence   Once a bureaucracy is created, it is virtually impossible to destroy it. It appropriates not only the individuals in its hierarchy but those it governs or serves to the extent that their continued economic and social existence depends upon the existence of the bureaucracy. What this means is that once the machinery of bureaucracy is set in motion and it reaches a size and scope which incorporates the technical specialties of a large number of individuals, we have created something that has, for all practical purposes, an existence of its own. Individuals at various levels of the hierarchy move in and out of office but the organization goes on. And, it goes on precisely for reasons I have discussed in Chapter 3. All the more or less self-oriented motivations of each individual involved are directed toward maintaining the organization, inasmuch as they perceive the survival of the organization as their own survival. The organization and their employment in it is their career, their status, their raison d'être, and may be their one channel for upward social mobility. The individual motivational systems of self-image maintenance, status maintenance, and reference group are the heartbeat of the organization.

Rationalization of Education   As a society becomes more and more marked by bureaucratization, traditional ideas about the purpose of education will change accordingly. Whereas the classic goal of education was to turn out a cultured man, the current goal is a trained specialist—an individual who has the technical knowledge which is a prerequisite for employment in the organization. In a democracy this has a revolutionary effect in that the gatekeepers of social prestige are no longer those with a monopoly of arbitrary wealth and power, but those with a monopoly of knowledge—the bestowers of diplomas, certificates of education, and special examinations. Predictably, the contemporary means for equality and social acceptability in the American society is the college degree. Weber also indicated (what foresight!) that as the volume of educational certificates and diplomas increases to fill all the slots in society with technically prepared specialists, the intellectual cost of education would decrease and the monetary costs increase.

Before going on to more contemporary analyses of modern formal organizations, the author would like to give Weber the last word in the inclusion of this lengthy but very interesting quotation.

We willingly admit that there are honourable and talented men at the top of our administration; that in spite of all the exceptions such people have opportunities to rise in the official hierarchy, just as the universities, for instance, claim that, in spite of all the exceptions, they constitute a chance of selection for talent. But, horrible as the thought is that the world may one day be peopled by professors—we would retire on to a desert island if such a thing were to happen—it is still more horrible to think that the world could one day be filled with nothing but those little cogs, little men clinging to little jobs and striving toward bigger ones— a state of affairs which is to be seen playing an ever-increasing part in the spirit of our present administrative system, and especially of its offspring, the students. This passion for bureaucracy, as we have heard it expressed here, is enough to drive one to despair.[3]

WORK, AND ITS MEANING IN A BUREAUCRATIC SOCIETY   Included in a relatively recent collection of readings that deals with the survival of the individual in mass society is an article by Joseph Bensman and Bernard Rosenberg which is particularly appropriate to our description of bureaucratic organization.[4]

[3] J. P. Mayer, *Max Weber and German Politics,* 2nd ed. (London: Faber and Faber, 1956), pp. 126–128.

[4] Joseph Bensman, and Bernard Rosenberg, "The Meaning of Work in Bureaucratic Society," in *Identity and Anxiety,* ed. Maurice Stein, et al. (Glencoe, Ill.: The Free Press, 1963), pp. 181–197. Adapted with permission of The Macmillan Company; © by The Free Press, a Corporation, 1960.

Their primary concern is with the subtle social-psychological effects upon the individual official, which have an eventual effect on the character of society when multiplied by each individual involved. Briefly, the conflicts concomitant with carrying out bureaucratic roles are the following:

1. Compulsive sociability.
2. Self-rationalization.
3. Disidentification.

As was indicated in an earlier chapter, the secondary relations which mark formal associations of people are marked by highly specific, contractual definitions of roles. People are judged by general standards which ignore personal-unique characteristics. This leads to a great deal of restraint and formality in social interactions. As such, these relations are the opposite of those in primary interactions, which are marked by very diffuse definitions of roles, much intimacy and judgments based on the unique aspects of each case. Primary relations are necessary for the development of integrated personalities as in the family and among peer groups. However, if they were the totality of all relations, it is assumed that social organization and the integration of society would suffer. On the other hand, if secondary relations had this totality of interpersonal activity, one would assume that personality development and integration of the self would suffer. This second assumption is the one specifically dealt with by Bensman and Rosenberg.

Compulsive sociability refers to the phenomenon of organizational norms that demand the outward characteristics of "amiability, sweet temper, and blandness." All other aspects of the official's personality must be kept hidden and controlled in that his continued employment, success, and advancement is dependent on only certain external behaviors being observed by others. Bensman and Rosenberg assume that after a time, control is no longer necessary—the official's personality becomes that which he externalizes and, as such, is that of an "Organization Man."

Self-rationalization refers to the process whereby the individual official takes the raw material of self and turns it into a marketable personality. The process is also referred to as adult socialization. The end product is a personality "totally in harmony with his environment." It is no coincidence that individuals in an organization appear to have observable traits that are very similar.[5]

Disidentification and overidentification are problems related to the effects of compulsive sociability and self-rationalization. Bensman and Rosenberg indicate, "In the midst of endless interaction with clients and other officials, the individual feels isolated, unbreakably tied to, and hopelessly cut off from those others he will see every working day of his life." One can appreciate the strains that may be concomitant with this. There are a number of alternative routes available to solve this strain, each of which has its effects upon both the organization and the official:[6]

1. Identity through primary attachments.
2. Identity outside of the bureaucracy.
3. Identity through the organization.

In an attempt to satisfy a need for primary interaction with others on a personal level, the official engages in activities that go beyond and/or are in conflict with his official role in the organization. The effect of this may satisfy certain personal needs and counter the effects of enforced sociability and self-rationalization, but the effect on the organization is not so fortunate, and long-range effects upon the individual and other officials may also be unfortunate. Bensman and Rosenberg make the assumption that such an existence of primary relations leads to the formation of informal cliques which may eventually superimpose their way of getting things done in the organization over the constitutional procedures. This flies in the face of rational structure, and efficiency suffers. Likewise, a new problem then faces the official—which clique will it be most politic to join?

Bensman and Rosenberg suggest that another alternative route is through "disidentification" with the bureaucracy. "Some bureaucrats, overwhelmed by the impersonality of their work, give up the idea that it is meaningful or that it is a suitable medium for self-realization. They turn to and enlarge upon other aspects of life,

[5] See Louis A. Zurcher, "The Sailor Aboard Ship," *Social Forces*, Vol. 43 (March, 1965), pp. 389–400.

[6] For another analysis of informal primary structures see Peter Blau, and Richard Scott, *op. cit.*, pp. 89–100.

while doing as little work as possible in offices that are distasteful to them."[7] Because their source of meaning is in other activities, they seek to perform only the minimum requirements of their office in a routine fashion, often passing the buck and decisions and problems upstairs to the next level of the hierarchy.

Some individuals solve the problems of identity by the employment of several techniques which associate self and job. Such techniques range from enmeshing themselves in the organizational womb to appropriating the bureaucracy for their own purposes. Through the use of the editorial "we" or "us" the individual can escape anonymity in the attempt of taking on the power and prestige of the organization as his own. For example, "We put out a great automobile this year," "We provide the best college education in the West," "We won the war," "We were instrumental in putting a man on the moon," etc., etc.

Another technique is through legalism, or rigid pursuance of the letter of the law. The precision or perceived precision of organizational rules provides great psychological security to the anonymous and powerless. Some may also go to the extreme of making the organization an extension of themselves, manipulating procedure for their own personal ends. Others may receive great comfort from exposing the incompetence and improper procedure of those in the hierarchy above them, or they may protect their offices and themselves by passing wrong information up and down the hierarchy, or by retaining information from another official.

SUMMARY

One would assume from taking into account what is discussed in this chapter that the bureaucratic organization is problematic for society and individuals, yet it is necessary in the light of our increased size, complexity, and technological development. Bensman and Rosenberg sum it up in this way:

> Real bureaucracy is neither as efficient as its ideal
> type suggests, nor as cruel and inefficient as our treat-

[7] Bensman, and Rosenberg, *op. cit.,* p. 187.

ment of its pathologies suggest. Not all people are frustrated by bureaucracy—toward which they may have gravitated by predisposition. No bureaucracy is exclusively staffed by pathological types. The negative characteristics we have sketched are, however, as much a reality as the positive ones. These tendencies pose typical problems and present typical difficulties which most white collar workers encounter at one time or another in the course of their careers.[8]

[8] *Ibid.*, p. 197.

Chapter 9   The Sociology of Deviant Behavior

This chapter will deal with sociological approaches to a variety of behaviors that are in one sense or another outside the societal prescriptions for behavior. Such behavior patterns are generally referred to as deviant, or in certain specific situations, as criminal or delinquent. As such, this area of sociological concern covers topics from miscellaneous sins to rape and homicide—a very broad area indeed—where distinctions sometimes become grey and blurred. The author will attempt to make such distinctions as are necessary without going off into airy flights of sociologism. Let's begin by defining some recurrent concepts in the discussions of deviant behavior, some of which may be familiar to you.

NORMS, NORMATIVE BEHAVIOR   Generally, norms refer to behaviors which are normal, prescribed, proscribed, expected, or anticipated. In one sense, normative behavior refers to correct role behavior for its associated status. In another sense, it refers to behavior which is predictable in the context of a particular situation. It also refers to behavior which is within the bounds of some shared group or societal definition of how one should act and react, such as in "etiquette." In your reading you may find norms categorized into mores and folkways. This language is a bit archaic, but it refers to norms which deal with very important aspects of behavior—sex, private property, and personal safety (mores)—and norms which deal with less important aspects of behavior, as table manners, speech, dress, personal hygiene (folkways). Now to the next concept.

Sanctions, Positive and Negative   Essentially, sanction refers to either reward or punishment that is forthcoming from others in the group when the individual enacts a particular behavior pattern. No doubt you are reading this in private, but suppose you were surrounded by observers just now when you picked your nose. Had it been that these observers were of a particular cultural background which regarded such activity highly, they may have paid you a compliment for your agility and deftness (positive sanction). On the other hand, had the group been comprised of typical American middle class members, they might have censured you for such activity, warning you that continued nasal digitation could jeopardize future group interaction (negative sanction). So it is with most behaviors that are enacted. In this case, we have been talking about the violation of a folkway. Had the behavior been one of violating a mos (singular for mores), the negative sanction would have been one of great severity. Heads would roll, as the saying goes.

Culture, Subculture   In sociological circles,[1] culture usually refers to the shared values, attitudes, language, and other traits of a people, society, or group. As such it is the set of meanings that people attach to the things and symbols in their shared environment. Subculture refers to a culture within a culture. For instance, certain cultural traits, like the English language, are universal in

[1] Two or more sociologists sitting around a pitcher of local brew.

American society. However, certain other traits are found only among certain ethnic or regional groups or economic classes, as varied dialects of the English language, differing religious preferences, ideas about moral behavior, etc. Such regional, ethnic or class specific things are subcultural traits. Such regions, ethnic or class groups are sometimes referred to as subcultures.

Deviant Behavior, Nonnormative Behavior   Essentially, deviant or nonnormative behavior is behavior that is defined by observers of that behavior as being outside the range of society's or the group's acceptable or prescribed (demanded or desired) behaviors at this time and place or for the status or identity of the person who is behaving. The individual who is enacting the behavior might be judged as performing a nonnormative act by the group collectively or by some specified member or members of the group whose role is that of moral watchdog (clergy, police, judges, referees, umpires, etc.).

Criminal Behavior[2]   Criminal behavior refers to deviant behavior of a specific type, that is to say, behavior which is in violation of highly specific norms of a society or group. Such norms are formulated as laws, codes, or statutes. A criminal is then a deviant whose behavior has been observed by a witness and is alleged to be illegal. If the individual is apprehended, tried, and found guilty, he receives the sanction prescribed by law.

CURRENT EXPLANATIONS OF DEVIANT AND CRIMINAL BEHAVIOR   This section will deal with a few of the more cogent and best known explanations of deviance in sociology. As in previous chapters, the coverage of these approaches will be in the form of simplified sketches and profiles. It is hoped that those theorists covered will accept our apologies for any short-changing of their works. The explanatory approaches to be sketched for you are these:

1. Subcultural theory and other typological approaches.
2. Opportunity theory and anomie.

[2] See Howard S. Becker, *The Outsiders* (New York: The Free Press, 1963).

3. Group dynamics and differential association theory.
4. Remarks on extra chromosomes.
5. Deviants by definition.

SUBCULTURAL THEORY AND OTHER TYPOLOGICAL APPROACHES Probably the best known use of subcultural concepts is by Albert Cohen in his analysis of juvenile delinquency. Such an approach has also been employed in the analysis of nearly everything from alcoholism to the generation gap. However, in the eyes of the author, Cohen's work presents the most plausible and understandable use of the concepts. Therefore, what follows is a profile of Cohen's subcultural theory. Extensions into other deviant areas should be readily grasped by the reader once Cohen is understood.

In *Delinquent Boys: The Culture of the Gang* the basic premises of Cohen's analysis are found.[3] In turn, some more contemporary extensions of these premises regarding adult criminal behavior are found in Clinard and Quinney's *Criminal Behavior Systems.*[4] In both of these works we find emphasis on the idea that there is a need for a general theory of deviance which fits the mountains of data about various types of deviance accumulating in the discipline. Moreover, certain traditional myths about deviant behavior are questioned and disposed of, namely, (1) the myth of deviance as the result of "bad blood," and (2) bad situations always lead to bad people. In general, we have finally made the quite obvious realization that deviant behavior results from the same social, psychological, and cultural processes which produce normal behavior.

Now, we will look at the basic premises lifted out of Cohen's theory of subcultures and elaborate just exactly what distinguishes a deviant subculture from any other kind of subculture. Here is how Cohen's argument develops:[5]

---

[3] Albert K. Cohen, *Delinquent Boys: The Culture of the Gang* (Glencoe, Ill.: The Free Press, 1964). Adapted with permission of The Macmillan Company; © by The Free Press, a Corporation, 1955.

[4] Marshall Clinard, and Richard Quinney, *Criminal Behavior Systems* (New York: Holt, Rinehart and Winston, 1967).

[5] Cohen, *op. cit.,* pp. 50–72.

Psychogenic Assumptions[6]

1. All human action is an ongoing series of efforts to solve problems.
2. Problems involve, until they are resolved, a certain tension, a disequilibrium, and a challenge.
3. Not every act is a successful solution. Not every problem is a bedevilment.
4. Most problems are familiar and recurrent.
5. What people do depends on the problems they contend with.
6. Such problems either come from the person's "frame of reference" or the "situation" he confronts.
7. Really hard problems are those for which we have no ready-at-hand solutions which will not leave us without feelings of tension, frustration, resentment, guilt, bitterness, anxiety, or hopelessness.
8. A really satisfying solution must (therefore) entail some change in that frame of reference itself.

Ecological Assumptions[7]

1. Human problems are not distributed in a random way among the roles that make up a social system.
2. Each category (racial, age, sex, ethnic, occupational, economic class) consists of people who have been equipped by their society with frames of reference and confronted by their society with situations which are not equally characteristic of other social roles.

Interaction Assumptions

1. Any solution that runs counter to the strong interests or moral sentiments of those around us invites punishment or the forfeiture of satisfactions which may be more distressing than the problem with which it was designed to cope.
2. Our dependence on our social milieu provides us with a strong incentive to select our solutions from among those

---

[6] Psychogenic: has its beginnings in the psychological structure.

[7] Ecological: has to do with the environmental system in which man lives.

already established and known to be congenial to our fellows.

3. More specifically, the consistency of our own conduct and of the frame of reference on which it is based with those of our fellows is a criterion of status and a badge of membership.

4. Not only recognition as members of some social category but also the respect in which others hold us are contingent upon the agreement of the beliefs we profess and the norms we observe with their norms and beliefs.

5. Not only is consensus rewarded by acceptance, recognition, and respect, it is probably the most important criterion of the validity of the frame of reference which motivates and justifies our conduct.

Subcultural Assumptions

1. The crucial condition of new cultural forms is the existence, in effective interaction with one another, of a number of actors with similar problems of adjustment.

2. The process is one of mutual conversion.

3. The emergence of these "group standards" of this shared frame of reference is the emergence of a new subculture.

4. Individuals will respond giving priority to subcultural norms instead of to major societal norms because . . . our ability to achieve status depends upon the criteria of status applied by our fellows, that is, the standards and norms they go by in evaluating people.

5. Individuals who share problems (will) gravitate toward each other and jointly establish new norms, new criteria for status which define as meritorious the characteristics they *do* possess.

6. The continued serviceability and, therefore, the viability of a subcultural solution entails the emergence of a certain amount of group solidarity and heightened interaction among participants in the subculture.

There you have it. When all these conditions are met, voila! a subculture emerges. Such a subculture may have normative standards and criteria for status achievement very similar to those of society at large, except in matters of dress, food, and language, and, therefore, may be considered nothing more than quaint. Others may differ to the point of being a threat to existing societal normative structures and would then be considered deviant, criminal, or delinquent.

OPPORTUNITY THEORY AND ANOMIE Richard Cloward and Lloyd Ohlin present another contemporary approach in their book, *Delinquency and Opportunity.*[8] This approach is not really different from that of Cohen's; rather it is an extension of analysis which goes beyond the description of subculture and makes a more specific statement of the "problems" that Cohen was talking about. A good part of the book is taken up with the repetition of the basic subcultural assumptions; however, much more explicit attention is given to the notion of delinquent norms which arise in the subculture with some specific reasons given for the emergence of these normative structures. Moreover, some specific delineations between differing types of delinquent norm structures are presented. The authors divide delinquent subcultures into three distinct types which are "typically found" when adolescent gangs are analyzed. They then make their unique contribution by wedding these subcultural concepts to Robert K. Merton's notions of anomie, the outcome of which is the so-called, Theory of Differential Opportunity. This theory implies both the differential access to legitimate means and the differential access to illegitimate means for acquiring the paramount material and status goals of our society. This, no doubt, leaves the uninitiated reader out in the cold. It would, therefore, be a good idea to present briefly Merton's notions regarding adaptation to an anomic social structure.

Merton's analysis begins with the assumption that contemporary industrial society in twentieth century America has certain structural characteristics which produce a condition of anomie.[9]

---

[8] Richard A. Cloward, and Lloyd E. Ohlin, *Delinquency and Opportunity* (Glencoe, Ill.: The Free Press, 1960).

[9] Robert K. Merton, *Social Theory and Social Structure,* 6th ed. (Glencoe, Ill.: The Free Press, 1962), pp. 131–160. Adapted with permission of The Macmillan Company. Copyright © 1957 by The Free Press, a Corporation. Copyright © 1949 by The Free Press.

This is to say that a certain disjunction exists between the ends and the means of utilitarian human actions within the collective. Or, as Merton puts it:

> Our primary aim is to discover how some social structures exert a definite pressure upon certain persons in the society to engage in nonconforming rather than conforming conduct.[10]

The focus of this discovery is upon the relationship between "cultural goals" (success or status items) and "institutionalized norms" (means for obtaining these goals about which there is some consensus). When certain conditions are not met in the relationship between goals and norms, anomie exists. When an individual seeks to adapt to this anomic condition there are certain probabilities that the adaptive behavior is deviant behavior. To enlarge on this, in such a society where goals and norms are not integrated in an effective manner (where great emphasis is placed on the goals but little concern is given to making the means for their acquisition available to all societal members), individuals will adapt a variety of ways depending on their individual characteristics (social and psychological). One characteristic is, of course, what Cloward and Ohlin refer to as differential access to the legitimate success means. Thus, in contemporary America, unless you are identifiable as having certain economic status, certain racial characteristics, and certain educational attainments, you may not have access to the legitimate routes for obtaining the goals by which success is measured, and if you should desire such success goals, you might then be required to use another route (usually illegitimate).[11]

If you're caught, you are a criminal; if you make it to home base without being caught (become a success), you may then be considered a good businessman. However, that is not the only

<hr/>

[10] *Ibid.*, p. 132.

[11] For example, where great emphasis is placed on higher education as a means to material success, access to higher education is not made available to all members of society, particularly to the lower class; individuals in the lower class may seek illegitimate means to achieve material success, such as pimping, hustling, membership in a syndicate, etc.

adaptation to the means-ends disjunction or anomie. Merton indicates that individuals will enact adaptive role behavior of a type consistent with a number of other variables. Those who have access to the legitimate means will use these and be conformists. Before discussing this idea further, it would be helpful to look at Merton's various adaptive types. In the following table "+" (plus) means that the norm or goal is accepted and "−" (minus) means that the norm or goal is rejected. A rejection and a substitution is indicated by "±".[12]

Mode of Role Behavior Adaptation (not a personality type)	Cultural Goals	Institutionalized Norms
1. Conformity (Squares)	+	+
2. Innovation (Hustlers)	+	−
3. Ritualists (Camps: virtue is its own reward)	−	+
4. Retreatists (Beats) (Hermits)	−	−
5. Rebellion (Rebels) (Revolutionaries)	±	±

GROUP DYNAMICS AND DIFFERENTIAL ASSOCIATION THEORY

Cohen's ideas about delinquent subcultures were greatly influenced by the works of the late Edwin Sutherland, to whom Cohen pays homage.[13] Cohen was impressed, no doubt, not only by Sutherland's hopes for a general theory of criminality, but also by

---

[12] Merton, *op. cit.,* p. 140.

[13] Albert Cohen, ed., *The Sutherland Papers* (Bloomington: The Indiana University Press, 1956).

Sutherland's explicit assumptions about the social-psychology of criminality.[14]

Sutherland indicates that we may state a scientific explanation of criminality either in terms of things operating during the occurrence of the crime (situational) or in terms of things operating in the history of the criminal (genetic). Of the two, he gives priority to the genetic approach, which means that when the necessary conditions are met in the genetic process a crime will occur, assuming a situation exists in which a crime could be committed.

Sutherland's theory, called differential association, is developed on the basis of the following assumptions. Note especially how these assumptions form a foundation for Cohen's work.

1. Criminal behavior is learned.

2. Criminal behavior is learned in interaction with other persons in communication.

3. The principal part of the learning of criminal behavior occurs within intimate personal groups. (Note: like any other kind of behavior.)

4. When criminal behavior is learned, the learning includes first, techniques of committing the crime, which are sometimes very complicated, sometimes very simple; and second, the specific direction of motives, drives, rationalizations, and attitudes.

5. The specific direction of motives and drives is learned from the definitions of legal codes as being favorable or unfavorable.

6. A person becomes delinquent because of an excess of definitions favorable to violation of law over definitions unfavorable to violation of law.

7. Differential associations may vary in frequency, duration, priority, and intensity.

8. The process of learning behavior by association with criminal and anticriminal patterns involves all of the mecha-

---

[14] Sutherland's "A Sociological Theory of Criminal Behavior" appears as Chapter IV in Sutherland and Cressey's *Principles of Criminology*, which was first published in the 1930s and which has been a standard sociology text for some years. Edwin Sutherland, and Donald Cressey, *Principles of Criminology*, 6th ed. (New York: J. B. Lippincott, 1960), pp. 74–81.

nisms that are involved in other learning. (Note: Prisons and universities may have a great deal in common.)

9. While criminal behavior is an expression of general needs and values, it is not explained by those general needs and values since noncriminal behavior is an expression of the same needs and values. (Note: This last assumption might be taken to task by Cohen who sees some criminality as being nonutilitarian and by Clinard who posits differential access to means and ends.)

REMARKS ON EXTRA CHROMOSOMES The preceding social-psychological-cultural approaches to the problem of deviance represent a contemporary breakthrough of sorts into the mysteries of abnormal behavior. Because we have lived with these notions of human behavior for a generation or more, students do not find them to be revolutionary ideas, but a short half-century ago the proponents of these kinds of ideas were generally deemed heretics by the scientific community.

At the turn of the century, and for some years prior to that, the initial assumption of investigators of deviant behavior was that criminal types are born, not made. On the heels of advances being made in biology (Darwin) and in psychology (Freud) were criminological "theorists" who sought to apply these new principles of science to a problem that had never really been solved in all of man's history. This application was not only premature, it was also accomplished by individuals who, although influenced by the scientific tenor of the times, were not sophisticated spokesmen. Thus sociology and criminology were set back. These men attempted to solve the problem of the explanation of deviance using principles of genetics, mildly spiced with Freudian psychology.

In short, a typical criminal was characterized as a genetic throwback—a Neanderthal with a midget superego. The most famous of such criminologists was Cesare Lombroso, who listed the physical traits or stigmata by which criminals might be easily recognized. Among these were protruding occipital ridges, low foreheads, small ears, weak chins, etc. Such characteristics were sure signs of antisocial types. Had this approach persisted,

Humphrey Bogart would never have been a believable bad guy. Treatises on bad blood and bad genes were legion. Some of these still persist, but as early as 1915 or so the phrenologists and social evolutionists became the heretics and criminology began to develop along the lines discussed in the earlier sections of this chapter.

Interestingly enough, the very latest fashion in criminological circles is again—yes, you guessed it—genetics. This time, however, the genetic concern is accompanied by better research techniques and the added assumptions of learning theory and subcultural conditioning. Lawyers are pleading cases using chromosome types as the defense. Researchers are finding higher rates of certain chromosome types in our prisons than in the normal population (significantly higher but not drastically higher). However, in the mid-twentieth century such findings are dealt with from a more sophisticated perspective, and as such, are quite consistent with our existing assumptions about social, psychological, and cultural variables.

One of the better coverages of this fairly recent development is that given by Ashley Montague in "Chromosomes and Crime" in the October, 1968 edition of *Psychology Today*.[15] No claim is given that genetics, and specifically chromosome anomalies, afford a sufficient explanation for criminality. The suggestion is that genetic anomaly may explain the criminality of about 3-to-4 per cent of our prison population. It should be noted, however, that the genetic characteristic alone does not explain this.

Specifically, most violent crimes are committed by normal individuals with normal chromosomes (XY). They are, after all, the most numerous in the population. But the high frequency with which XYY individuals commit crimes of violence indicates that the extra Y chromosome exerts an effect in influencing aggressive behavior.

How does this work? Is it a genetically predetermined action, or does the genetic programming of growth and development create an individual who, by virtue of his physical characteristics, is constantly defined by others as different and an outsider?

[15] Ashley Montague, "Chromosomes and Crime," *Psychology Today* (October, 1968).

Montague lists the following as characteristics typically found in XYY chromosome individuals.

1. Among these types there is a high incidence of abnormal genitalia.
2. Such individuals are usually strikingly tall, even in child-hood.
3. Facial acne appears to be frequent in adolescence.
4. IQ's are rather low (80–95).
5. There is a high probability of an epileptic condition.
6. Usually there are disorders of the teeth (discoloration, etc.).

It is no stretch of the imagination to assume that such individuals are going to stand out as being different from their peers and siblings and as such are going to receive differential response from others, a good deal of which is going to be negative. Now, read again the initial topics of this chapter and the ideas about socialization in the earlier chapters. How would you predict the life chances for legitimate activity in regard to XYY individuals?

DEVIANTS BY DEFINITION   The work of Howard S. Becker has become a benchmark in the literature of deviance, not so much be-cause it is a completely new approach, but because it puts a new twist to the concepts already discussed above. Published in 1963, *The Outsiders* represents a rearrangement of well-used concepts in such a way as to provide for a fresh look at the situational aspects of the deviant.

> It is easily observable that different groups judge differ-ent things to be deviant. This should alert us to the possibility that the person making the judgment of deviance, the process by which the judgment is arrived at, and the situation in which it is made may all be inti-mately involved in the phenomenon of deviance.[16]

Becker shifts our attention from the deviant to situations and others which label the individual in question as deviant. Such a shift opens up new vistas in that we can no longer be so confident

[16] Becker, *op. cit.*, p. 4.

in assuming that acts of rule-breaking are inherently deviant. There are linguistic and cultural dimensions here that have been overlooked.

Likewise, some of our subcultural concerns can shift from the subculture of deviance to the subculture of "moral entrepreneurs," another minority which possibly defines a range of acts as deviant and is in position to enforce such definitions. Such an idea existed for some time in European jurisprudence (unpopular as the idea was), but Becker introduced it into American criminology. He does not mince words in doing this. "Social groups create deviance by making the rules whose infraction constitutes deviance."[17]

Some corollaries of making this first assumption (deviance by label) are then thrust upon us, as Becker indicates, in that we next assume that the degree to which definers react to a given act will depend upon: (1) changes in attitudes about the act over time, (2) who or what kind of individual commits the act, (3) attitudes about the consequences of the act.[18]

We must also assume that behavior is behavior. The same determinants of normal behavior are at work in much of what is labeled deviant behavior. We add the adjective, deviant, to the noun, behavior, as a result of our own cultural prerogatives. "Differences in the ability to make rules and apply them to other people are essentially power differentials."

SUMMARY

For each characteristic society with its own peculiar authority pattern, explanations of order have been posited. The theocracy of the Middle Ages arose out of religious consensus, and moral behavior was based on fear of retribution or a desire for heavenly bliss. The rise of an industrial society saw the rise of theories that were based on what has been defined as contractual arrangements between the members of society as man gives up some individual

[17] *Ibid.,* p. 9.
[18] *Ibid.*

freedom and satisfaction in return for the benefits of group living. To break the contract results in punishment by the group.

Current theories of order seem to be of a deterministic nature, the major premises being concerned with the individual as a product of his particular cultural environment in that he is molded by his society and for his society. If this individual creation process is efficient, society will have solidity as a result of this internalized motive on the part of the individual to engage in or refrain from behavior deemed moral or immoral by society. Cohesion will result from this built-in consensus. The responsibility of keeping order, therefore, rests with the cultural environment, and individual deviance is traced to some malfunction in the socialization process.

As noted, the deterministic theories of order and deviance may be in part under question. The more existential concerns for the relativity of values and linguistic designations may soon put deviance in an altogether new light.

Chapter 10   Emergence and Transformation of Society

Introduction

Some people think the mind is impotent to influence social affairs, others that it is omnipotent. Whilst I believe that the technological factors are important I should maintain that they be manoeuvred according to human ends which are culturally agreed. Or, as Lewis Mumford puts it, 'our capacity to go beyond the machine rests in our power to assimilate the machine.' In our advanced technical age it would be impossible to destroy the machine but it is possible with intelligence to remove those institutions which do harm, or strengthen those tendencies which are already at work and useful but not fully developed. Social reform does not mean building society anew from the beginning, but observing the tendencies at work and through a definite strategy guiding it in the desired direction.[1]

Society used to be viewed as a state of nature whose attributes did or did not change in accordance with supernatural designs or other forces similarly unknown to and uncontrolled by man. This conception of society has gradually been modified; it is now more widely viewed as in principle given to deliberate restructuring in accord with the values of its members.[2]

For the existence of any science, it is necessary that there exist phenomena which do not stand isolated. In a world ruled by a succession of Miracles performed by an irrational God subject to sudden whims, we should be forced to await each new catastrophe in a state of perplexed passiveness.[3]

Western man is now well into the era of social guidance. It is upon changing society now that man is directing his intelligence and technology. As the saying goes, "It is better late than never." Perhaps this emphasis has been long in arriving because until now man's energies have been directed toward controlling his physical environment, which of necessity takes precedence. It may be that careful planning for the good society was never before needed or perceived as being needed. At any rate, social change in the history of man's existence has been left primarily to spontaneous transformation and it is through transformation—evolution, migration, conflict, accumulation, and revolution—that modern societies have emerged. Rather than being the conscious handiwork of man they were the by-products of his struggle for survival. Surely, these processes of change continue to operate, but with increased knowledge about human needs and societal requisites change is becoming planned change. This is a new imperative of species survival.

[1] Karl Mannheim, *Systematic Sociology* (New York: Grove Press, 1964), p. 139.

[2] Sarajane Heidt, and Amitai Etzioni, eds., *Societal Guidance: A New Approach to Social Problems* (New York: Thomas Y. Crowell, 1969), pp. 5 and 6.

[3] Norbert Wiener, *Cybernetics,* as quoted by Don Fabun, *The Dynamics of Change* (Englewood Cliffs, N. J.: Prentice-Hall, 1968), Part IV, p. 21.

Cities can no longer grow like Topsy. Wars for the sake of honor or acquisition or ideology are suicidal. Racial and ethnic differences can no longer be the criteria for division of labor or division of goods. The conflicts between the scientific revolution and humanism are, at last, having their effects upon social phenomena. Before discussing this notion of social guidance further, it would be well to elucidate the spontaneous processes of societal emergence and transformation mentioned above.

Evolution   There are three aspects of societal evolution which must be differentiated, keeping in mind that they are all bound together in the process of change: bio-evolution, techno-evolution, and cultural-evolution. They are inseparable, each being dependent upon and reinforcing the other. They are triggered by the necessity of adaptation to a world that from the beginning has been hostile to this nonspecialized creature known as Homo Sapiens.

Ever since man was "cast out of Eden," he has spent his energies in attempting to create a new paradise on earth. Only of late, however, have his architectural energies toward this end been conscious. To put it another way, the inventions and institutions of contemporary man are the result of a historical neurosis urging man's survival even in an unsympathetic environment. Bio-evolution, of course, refers to the process of genetic evolution which has brought into existence man as a particular kind of biological creature. Techno-evolution refers to the development of the use of tools by man—implements which are extensions of his less-than-adequate muscles, ranging from sharp-edged rocks to lunar modules. Cultural-evolution refers to the development of values and institutions in human societies concomitant with technological development and human evolution.

As indicated above, the three types of evolutionary change are dependent upon each other. The organism had to develop biologically to a certain level of complexity before it could psychologically perceive the link between a rock and its use in performing a task that was impossible with the arm and hand alone. Likewise, once an arsenal of crude tools was available to simplify the survival struggle of the species this, no doubt, had an effect on the selection and adaptation processes which determined the continued biological evolution of the organism. The fit who survived and reproduced were those who mastered the tools of survival. Some specialized organisms became extinct when the environment changed, Homo Sapiens adapted and evolved. Likewise, as the tool-making activity increased, the social aspects of man's behavior developed. Norms, values, and institutions of family, religion, economics, politics, and science are also survival adaptations. Modes of control and social order developed with increasing complexity as technology and the size of populations increased. This type of social change one considers to be nonconscious or spontaneous in that it occurs without rational human plan. The development of some aspect of technology may be purposive and conscious, but its concomitant social-cultural consequences are not intended or foreseen. It is only in the last century that mankind has sought to analyze this relationship and attempt to predict social and biological consequences in its technology. And it has been only a couple of decades that we have seriously considered the need to guide the shape of the future by the application of knowledge gained from this analysis. We hope to make our technology work for us instead of becoming slaves to it. For instance, the various inventions culminating in the automobile have consequences for Americans in the 1970s that are undesirable. One cannot escape the fact that the automobile has had tremendous and irreversible impact on our social situation. Soon that will be history. Are we prepared for the social impact of micro-miniaturized circuitry and the servo-mechanisms they make possible? Can we live comfortably with robots and the voice of mission control?

Migration Another mechanism of emergence is migration and the intercultural contacts it provides. The migratory movements of people have played an important part in the emergence of civilization and continue to affect changing societies. Whether such movements are within or between societies, they greatly enhance the rate of social change and the accumulation of cultural attributes. These cultural contacts, be they benign or bellicose, bring about new syntheses of thought, technological innovation, religious ideology, or philosophy. To cite a recent example, think for a moment about American and Russian developments in space technology in relation to postwar migration (voluntary and otherwise) of German physicists and technicians. Or, going back a bit further, migration (forced as it was) from Africa affected the uniquely American innovations that range from jazz to peanut butter. And, if one lets his imagination go, could it possibly be that the Texas barbecue is the offspring of the Swedish smorgasbörd and the Mexican fiesta. Then, on a more microscopic level of intra-societal migration, notice that the country music of Nashville is big in Los Angeles and that chitlins and greens are big in Detroit.

The author puts great importance on the link between diffusion of cultural entities and migration because it has not been until recently that increased literacy and increased sophistication of mass media technology have made the diffusion of ideas without contact possible. With Telstar the diffusion of the content of inter-cultural exchange will be more controlled and specific. In the past such exchanges have been quite spontaneous depending upon what kinds of people migrated and for what reasons.

The cultural diffusion which results from movements of people, be they farmers, exiles, or soldiers, and whether or not the contact is one of conflict or cooperation, is an important aspect of the emergence and transformation of civilization. One can imagine that if the various cultures of the world had been isolated in some manner for the last 30,000 years each would have crystalized at some point regarding technology, religion, etc., developing no further. Those few isolated cultures which existed until the nineteenth century were quite primitive and had existed unchanged for a great period of time.

Conflict   Another determinant of societal dynamics is conflict and the means by which conflict is resolved. Such conflict may be that which takes place between societies or that which takes place within societies between economic-political interest groups or between racial-ethnic groups. Likewise, it exists on many levels and takes many forms. Most of the time we equate conflict with violence, war, or destruction, but these phenomena represent only one level of conflict. Unless there are established modes within the structure of society for venting steam, or unless there exist institutionalized means of conflict resolution, violence is the level that resolution will take. As man moves into the era of societal guidance and planned change, mechanisms of conflict resolution will have high priority.

A number of examples of intra- and inter-societal conflict can be given: (1) intellectual conflict—argument, debate—often results in the creation of new ideas; (2) economic conflict—competition in the marketplace—often leads to the creation of new technology, new products, and more egalitarian forms of distribution; (3) political conflict—if resolved through egalitarian procedures—can lead to a greater good for a greater number; and (4) ethnic and racial conflict, when peaceably resolved, can result in rich exchanges between cultures.

On an international level, the United Nations and its mechanisms represent an attempt at worldwide conflict resolution. Labor-management mediation boards represent attempts to institutionalize conflict resolution among societal interest groups. The problem is one of allowing for the existence of conflict, yet, at the same time, retaining a means of control which can intercede before it reaches a destructive level.

Should a society deny the operation of these modes of conflict-resolution, there are two logical results: (1) stagnation and crystallization of the social and cultural structure resulting in an anthill society such as in *Brave New World,* or (2) the cumulation of pressures to a critical point resulting in an eruption of violence and revolution.

Revolution   Like many concepts dealt with in sociology, the term, revolution, has several usages in common and technical language. Generally speaking, in socio-political jargon it refers to a rapid and violent change in the social structure. Sometimes it is incorrectly used as a synonym for social change as in "the sexual revolution" or "revolution in the classroom," which tends to soften the ominous tone of the word. Revolution as a mode of change usually exacts an exorbitant price in lives and property and an extended lack of order. But then, high as the price is, there have been many times throughout history when this mode of change has appeared as the only recourse to a people shackled by the chains of tradition.

With this in mind, the author presents the following general sketch of the process revolutions usually follow. This sketch represents recurrent and general themes in a variety of literature which deals with revolution. The author's views are heavily affected by the works of Crane Brinton and by a series of lectures on this topic presented by Professor Virgil Williams at Washington State University in the early 1960s.

The sociological indicators of the stage of social unrest are usually one or a number of the following conditions: (1) rising aspirations and expectations which are not met, (2) contacts with other societies which reinforce dissatisfactions, (3) perceived moral decay, (4) weak government or alienation from the processes of government, and (5) anomie. It is not so much the effects of unequal distribution of economic goods and power which leads to disaffection, but the fact that an observable gap exists between the *aspirations* for goods and power and what a people are actually able to achieve.

The condition of widespread unrest usually leads to some kind of analgesic reaction, the purpose of which is simply to relieve the psychological tensions of the shared unrest. In times of uncertainty, not knowing the exact cause of their distress, people will act to relieve the stress anyway. During the plagues in Europe people would dance in the streets until exhausted or select one of their group as a witch and have a witch burning to expiate the source of their distress. During times of social unrest such crowd behavior is observable in the forms of rioting, demonstrations, sporadic burning and looting, or simply dancing, singing, and sharing each other's testimonials of displeasure. A crowd sharing such experiences on repeated occasions forms what we call sectarian associations. In these sectarian associations are the embryos of anything from new religious denominations to political parties to criminal syndicates. Such embryos can become almost any kind of organization over time, and, depending on their nature, they hold the seeds for either reforms which solve the aspiration-achievement problem or a revolution that accomplishes the same at a higher price.

The second phase begins when there occurs a crucial shift in the allegiance of the intellectuals and of the society from the elites to the non-elites, or disaffected elements. At this point the common man may be idolized in the writings, paintings, plays, and philosophies of the intelligentsia and a new social myth emerges. The myth, or ideology, describes the utopia to be won, it fuses the mystical bonds of the crowd and the ideas of the intellectuals, it damns the status quo and calls the committee to arms. As this second phase draws to its conclusion there is a coalition of the various sectarian associations into a united revolutionary front; this sets the stage for the third phase, the phase of the revolution or civil war.

The phase of civil war is marked by a splintering of the old social structure—boundaries of allegiance are drawn and sides are chosen. In most cases there are three factions, the conservatives or royalists, the moderates who have given up thoughts for reform, and the radicals whose revolution is finally at hand. The struggle for power ensues and through military action and reign of terror each faction seeks to win the day. Eventually, one faction is successful in putting down the others. More than likely, the moderates and the radicals have struck a coalition and have routed the old regime.

The victors must then face the undermined economy—scorched fields, rampant disease, and hunger. This, then, is the beginning of the final phase, the phase of institutionalization or reconstruction, often characterized by a compromise between revolutionary idealism and practical demands. Political purges are carried out against those who pose a threat to the new regime.

There is no final answer regarding the efficacy of any revolution, but the relative merits of the revolutions which most western societies have experienced in the past 200 years are often debated. Some consider revolution a sociopathic abnormality, society always being worse off for it. Others feel that the good wrought for the following generations is worth the cost of lives and properties involved; that it was the only choice in an intolerable situation. But then different revolutions have different costs. There are even those who would argue that revolution is the only way to effect thorough changes in society. In the age of space technology such people seem strangely archaic. Or do they?

Part II   Social Systems and Societal Enterprises

Chapter 11 Introduction to the Idea of Systems

Part I of this book dealt with the general problem of weaving the individual into the web of society. It was an attempt to (1) describe the way in which individuals act in concordance to form a social structure, (2) describe the nature of that structure, and (3) show how the structure in turn acts upon individual humans.

In the next four chapters, the author will portray society as an ongoing, dynamic system by showing how its basic subsystems in interplay create the whole. The concern will not be with the socio-psychological concepts of Part I, but will focus on structures and processes which have the appearance of transcending human action and interaction. In short, the concern will be with collective processes, i.e., the consequences of people acting collectively in systems. The final chapter in Part II will deal with a prognosis for the new directions sociology may take in research and conceptualization in seeking answers to questions now being raised regarding social systems. Before anything more is said, it would be well to note what a human social system is, or what is involved in a human system or collective enterprise. A history of the development of the systems approach could be a semester course in itself. As a methodological approach that aids in the understanding of the world around us the systems model has been an extremely productive device. Since its earliest use in classical astronomy and its subsequent formalization in the metaphysics of Kant and Hegel, the utility of systems thinking has been demonstrated in the conceptual breakthroughs of Darwin, Freud, Weber, and especially Einstein. The wide usage of the systems approach since the late nineteenth century by the "hard sciences" was engendered by the necessity to overcome the overpowering skepticism which was concomitant with sciences whose principles were based upon naive notions of simple one-way cause and effect ideas. Early in the Enlightenment period, David Hume demonstrated by argument that to assume "A" causes "B" simply because "A" and "B" are observed to be in proximity in time and space was fallacious. He argued that there were no logical or empirical ways to prove that the supposed relationship between variable factors was not spurious (i.e., an artifact of our limited sensory equipment).

The skepticism regarding knowledge based upon simplistic cause-effect thinking grew into cynicism. This cynicism was most profound among German idealists who saw the world as a much more complex totality than it was represented to be by naive determinism which was based on causality assumptions.

Out of this cynicism new approaches to modeling phenomena (including the social and physical) grew. One of the most prevalent approaches was that of organicism or structural-functional analysis as pioneered by Herbert Spencer. This approach saw society as being analogous metaphorically to a living organism. It wasn't long before this approach got out of hand with theorists referring to the "heart" of society or to society's "circulation." Who knows how far this could have gone before becoming downright scatological. As a result of the limited utility of metaphor, the functional organic approach became suspect.

Organismic concepts were an improvement over naive determinism in that they fostered an awareness of the interrelatedness of parts and gave ontological reality to the whole. However, organicism also created much theoretical and semantic confusion due to the grand metaphor itself.

With the work of Georg Simmel in the early twentieth century we find the first articulate expression of the idea that societies are not like something else. Societies are societies and must be understood on their own terms. Societies are not solar systems; societies are not biological systems; they are social systems. Therefore, with modern social systems approaches we keep the notion of an integrated whole of interdependent parts and we discard the language of metaphor as best we can. The important thing is that systems concepts do not depend on an epistemology of one-way cause and effect. All variable system units are interactive and interdependent and the outcome might be referred to as a social relativity theory.

Joseph Monane provides a most explicit definition in a recent book on social systems which offers a point of departure for our consideration.[1]

> The normal social system is composed of (1) components (people, artifacts, ideas, emotions) of varying manipulative power in regular nonrandom patterns of action with one another. This involves the (2) sending and receiving of energy/information among components of the system. The system is simultaneously involved in (3) sending and receiving energy/information with its (4) environments, including other systems. Its patterns of action within and with its environments, constitute (5) modal norms providing it with a distinctive identity. Its (6) power units, internally and in their action with the system environments seek (7) positive feedback implementing their directing of system action and resist (8) negative feedback impeding this action. (9) Change (arising within the system, or involving the inflow or outflow with its environment) that is perceived

[1] Joseph Monane, *The Sociology of Human Systems* (New York: Appleton-Century-Crofts, 1967), pp. 3–5.

by a system's power units as providing positive feedback is permitted and encouraged, while (10) change that is perceived as providing negative feedback is resisted internally through patterns of (11) expulsion, confinement, or conversion. Externally, such change is resisted by withdrawal, a tightening of gateways or a joining with it so as to remove its danger. (12) Change that succeeds in creating negative feedback produces varying degrees of (13) system disintegration. This, however, is rarely final. New systems spring up from old through (14) resystematization.[2]

Norman Storer treats systems a bit less abstractly and defines them in more human terms. His treatise implies the fourteen dimensions of systems made explicit by Monane, but it focuses on those most available and most necessary for our understanding of collecting enterprises.[3] Generally, his concern is with human systems as continuing processes of commodity creation, commodity exchange, and a normative structure which governs these. Both Monane and Storer imply constant change or dynamic flux in the notion of system. This is a departure from earlier functional concepts which sought to model systems and change on the basis of equilibrium notions. Keeping in step with nineteenth century physics, sociologists recognize equilibrium as a problem concept. A stalled airplane is in equilibrium, but the probability of immediate change is always high. It would be nice if systems stood still long enough for us to get a look at them, or at least if the various parts all changed in unison. But such is not the case. Only in abstracting the general boundaries and components of a system can we "get a fix on" its nature. Not only are systems in constant movement, but also the interfaces between systems are constantly in the process of change.

Robert Boguslaw's coverage of systems in *The New Utopians* adds no further dimension to the definitions that have already been entertained, but he does offer a warning about the implications of

[2] *Ibid.,* pp. 3–5.

[3] Norman Storer, *The Social System of Science* (New York: Holt, Rinehart and Winston, 1966), pp. 29–56.

thinking in terms of systems.[4] He states that one must be careful that the analytical model (the idea of system used to understand the nature of collective human enterprise) does not become a blueprint for engineered structures for the control of human enterprise and action.

With the above considerations in mind, the following is put forth as the structure by which the basic enterprises of modern society are to be analyzed in the following chapters:

1. The idea of systems and subsystems will form the framework for the analysis *keeping in mind that systems are abstractions* and that they are *devices used to aid understanding.*

2. For the present work, systems will be thought of as constellations of people who collectively produce some kind of commodity for greater society. These people receive rewards of one kind or another according to system definitions for the part they play in this enterprise, and they carry out their activities in ways consistent with the norms or the ethos of the system.

3. The characteristic norms of the system form its boundaries, the interface between systems, and the cohesive agent of systems. Likewise, the commodity produced is an identifier of a system.

Using the framework above allows for a practical use of the systems model in that the basic requirements of system-thinking are fairly well met as set down by Gustav Bergmann in his characterization of this construct as it is used in celestial astronomy:[5]

1. *Identification:* One must delimit a group of objects in a limited space that remain as an identifiable group over an appreciable length of time.

2. *Notation of Closure:* One must establish the boundaries of the system.

[4] Robert Boguslaw, *The New Utopians* (Englewood Cliffs, N. J.: Prentice-Hall, 1965).

[5] Gustav Bergmann, *Philosophy of Science* (Madison: University of Wisconsin Press, 1958), pp. 75–124.

3. *Inventory:* One must have knowledge of the relevant varible properties of the system.
4. *Stasis:* One must be able to observe and describe the state of a system at a particular time.
5. *Entropy:* One must then be able to note change in the system from one time to the next.

Such a model is very workable when analyzing the solar system, for example, but obviously we cannot meet these requirements perfectly when modeling social phenomena. In the case of the solar system all of the properties are measurable as physical entities and a description of change is definite and observable.

1. *Identification:* The sun, its planets and their respective moons.
2. *Closure:* The boundary is marked by the orbit of the last planet.
3. *Inventory:* Knowledge of the variables of mass, velocity, and gravitational attraction allow for an understanding of the phenomena in question.
4. *Stasis:* A description of the system at time x provides a static model of the system denoting placement of all the components vis-à-vis one another.
5. *Entropy:* The bodies in motion move according to laws and hence move predictably, changing position in relation to one another and the whole system according to an established pattern.

When Bergmann's approach is applied to social phenomena, its value is mainly in the insights it offers rather than in a strict and rigorous description. In addition, the value of this approach is maintained in proportion to the amount of skepticism the sociologist maintains relative to such an analytical framework.

The systems (subsystems) which interact to comprise the modern industrial societies—economy, politics, religion, and science—have been the focus of intense analysis and critique for the last 200 years or more. During the Enlightenment, philosophers such as Montesquieu and Rousseau had a rationalistic and humanistic concern for uncovering the mysteries of man's institutions. In the early nineteenth century the mode of analysis shifted to the positive empirical critique of Comte and St. Simon. In both cases, however, there was an academic recognition that human institutions are human products and ought to be designed for human purposes. Such utopian concerns became most explicit later in the works of Karl Marx, who was audacious enough to suggest the existence of a certain lawful progression in the evolution of human institutions, even to the point of predicting the nature of the end product of social change. In so doing he expressed man's creative part in the process and at the same time (contradictory in appearance) painted a picture of the historical process which grinds on according to the forces of destiny. The acceptance of this idea in European intellectual circles, the occurrence of disturbing ideas from the budding philosophy of existentialism, the sterile empiricism of actuarial economics, and the magic of fin de siècle coupled with the dry rot of ancien régimes necessitated a new positivism, a new empiricism; in short, a new sociological approach at once analytical and pragmatic.

The seeds of systematic analysis were sown at the century's turn in the genius of what some have called the Bourgeois Marxists—Max Weber, Emile Durkheim, and Vilfredo Pareto. In general, these were thinkers who sought to avert the crisis of western society by understanding the nature of the systems which interacted to produce the modern phenomena. Needless to say, the crisis was not averted. After the Russian Revolution and World War I, the post-crisis heirs of this intellectual tradition—Karl Mannheim, Pitirim Sorokin, and Talcott Parsons—maintained the grand analytical style, seeking again to understand and perhaps alleviate industrial society's ills.

From the work of these grand theorists, from the plethora of highly specific research that consciously or not seeks to verify hypotheses put forth by these theorists, certain conclusions can be drawn concerning the character of modern social systems and their growth trends as they relate in interface to each other and to the whole. Likewise, since the late fifties, there has been a certain impatience with either the lack of practical knowledge or the rate at which it accumulates. Such a state of affairs has brought into present sociology a school referred to as "new sociology"—a group of intellectuals, professors, and students who desire to implement our premature conclusions with all possible haste in order to save society and man from the pathologies elaborated by the Bourgeois Marxists and modern liberals—ecological crisis, population squeeze, nuclear disaster, inequality, genocide, alienation, meaninglessness, and repression in the complex total state. It is, therefore, with the concern of systems and system change that the second part of this work deals. It is an attempt to present something of relevance without the dripping self-pity of "Easy Rider" on the one hand, or the semantic retreatism of the *American Sociological Review* on the other. In so doing, the focus will be on the relationship between the basic enterprises of a modern society on the larger structural scale. These enterprises are often referred to as institutions in sociological literature, but there is much semantic confusion surrounding the concept of institutions. Generally, the notion of social institutions is defined as a cluster of norms, values, and behavior patterns which are related to a particular set of human goals. Then when these institutions are listed, the list usually includes everything from the family to political conventions, with some mention made of what function each plays in an ongoing society. Instead of using this approach, the present work will deal with relationships within and between the basic macroscopic enterprises or action systems which make up a society.

Briefly, an enterprise is a system of values (ethos), normative stipulations, status and role stipulations, and a set of goals which structure the actions of human beings who are collectively involved in the production and exchange of some set of commodities. The basic enterprise systems of society result in the attainment of societal goals and the structure of total society—order, legitimacy, production, distribution, and growth. The basic systems are: (1) the religious system, (2) the techno-scientific system, (3) the economic system, and (4) the politico-governmental system.

The religious enterprise is a system of actors ranging from officials within the religious establishment to poets, publicists, playwrights, and novelists who are involved in the production and/or reinforcement of ideals, ideologies, or the paramount moral distinctions of a society. In western industrial societies the general output of this enterprise has been defined by Max Weber as a moral prescription often termed Judeo-Protestant asceticism because of its aspects of practical efficiency, pietism, and pragmatism, or the puritan ethic.

The techno-scientific enterprise is a system of actors generally referred to as scientists, scholars, or engineers who adhere to a certain systemic structure in the production of a general set of commodities including certified knowledge, discovery of principles concerning the operation of the phenomenal world, and the application of this knowledge in invention and in the utilization of techniques to control and manipulate or simply understand nature for human benefit (or sometimes its converse).

The economic enterprise is a system of actors of a wide range of types whose collective action (within a set of prescriptions) results in a system output of goods and stipulations about their distribution.

The political enterprise is a set of actors in systemic relation of a wide range of types. The output of this system is the formalization and enforcement of societal-wide behavior stipulations (laws, codes, statutes, and constitutions) which insure the primacy of the current ideology as initially found in the religious enterprise. Also, in an integrated macrocosm it gives legitimacy to the action and output of the scientific and economic systems.

SUMMARY

The chapters in this part of the book will give exposition to the above definitions and these ideas will represent an attempt to show the interactions between these systems. In doing so, the author will utilize the concepts defined and enlarged upon in the first part of the text. These first introduced concepts are the building blocks used to construct a model of the greater society. Needless to say, the exposition will be incomplete—a rough outline. Its only purpose is to aid the student in perceiving society as an operating entity that has results and consequences which might be anticipated given our understanding of the processes. Given the accumulation of additional information in the forthcoming decades, this may be the last "accidental century."

Chapter 12   The Enterprise of Religion

The enterprise of religion either produces or reinforces the existing belief system or ideology of a total societal system. And, as we shall see, this really means that it affects all other systems.[1] In interface with science, politics, or economics the result will be either a positive or negative feedback which reinforces or affects the ethos and the acceptability of the product of the other system. Likewise, in order for the religious enterprise to maintain its existence as a system, it may join with another system by radically modifying its own ethos so as to remove the contradiction if, by chance, it cannot impress its existing ethos upon the system in question.

The rise of the scientific mentality in western history, or the

[1] See Joseph Monane, *The Sociology of Human Systems* (New York: Appleton-Century-Crofts, 1967).

so-called scientific revolution, has often been linked to the asceticism of the Calvinism-Lutheranism of the Reformation. However,
it might also be possible that the Reformation itself is an example
of the religious enterprise redesigning its ethos to parallel the
change going on in the enterprise of science and economics.

One could suggest that prior to and simultaneously with the
Protestant Reformation there were attempts by Catholic thinkers
either to make Catholic dogma acceptable to the new order or to
have it influence the direction of the new order itself. On the one
hand, St. Thomas Aquinas attempted to portray Catholic theology
as falling under the rubric of reason and logic, while on the other,
the theological experts of the Holy Office in Rome examined the
works of secular philosophers for their theological correctness.

> On 24 February 1616 the theological experts, or quali-
> fiers, of the Holy Office delivered their famous report.
> They reported that the proposition that 'the sun is the
> centre of the world and altogether devoid of local mo-
> tion' was 'foolish and absurd philosophically, and for-
> mally heretical, inasmuch as it expressly contradicts
> the doctrine of holy scripture in many places, both ac-
> cording to their literal meaning, and according to the
> common exposition and meaning of the Holy Fathers
> and Doctors.'[2]

By 1620 the ban on Copernican theory was lifted as long as the
books contained the correction that such a theory was a hypothesis only and not a true description as Galileo was wont to believe.
This is an example of system reintegration after negative feedback.

System Boundaries   What are the present system boundaries and
the products of the religious enterprise in western society? From
the works of Weber and Merton specifically, one is led to accept
three basic dimensions in the structure of the ethos of the religious enterprise: (1) pietism, (2) asceticism, and (3) puritanism,
which together form the Protestant Ethic. As a boundary of the

[2] Alistair C. Crombie, *Medieval and Early Modern Science,* Vol. II, 2nd ed.
(Cambridge: Harvard University Press, 1961), p. 211.

system of religion, the Protestant Ethic has been best described by Max Weber in the following summary statement of Weber's description of Calvinism provided by Raymond Aron.

1. There exists an absolute, transcendent God who created the world and rules it, but who is incomprehensible, inaccessible to the finite minds of men.

2. This all powerful and mysterious God has predestined each of us to salvation or damnation, so that we cannot, by our works, alter divine decree which was made before we were born.[3]

3. God created the world for his own glory.

4. Whether he is to be saved or damned, man is obliged to work for the glory of God and to create the Kingdom of God on earth.

5. Earthly things,[4] human nature, and the flesh belong to the order of sin and death, and salvation can come to man only through divine grace.[5]

Now, let us translate from Calvinist dogma to religious ethos and find the dimensions of the boundaries of the religious system which are in interface with the other systems in society.

Pietism   A dimension that marks one of the revolutionary shifts of Reformation belief from the belief system of pre-Reformation Catholicism is that of pietism. It marks a shift from group or collective worship and definition of God to individual definition and worship of God. The consequence of this shift is that it is an individual's responsibility to work out his own salvation. It marks the encroachment of individualism into the collectivistic nature of the Mass and the confessional. Joachim Wach sees pietism as the

---

[3] Irving Zeitlin includes here the quotation from Weber that "it is an absolute duty to consider one's self chosen, and to combat all doubts as temptations of the devil, since lack of self-confidence is the result of insufficient faith, hence of perfect grace." Irving Zeitlin, *Ideology and the Development of Sociological Theory* (Englewood Cliffs, N. J.: Prentice-Hall, 1968), p. 227.

[4] This should be read as: earthly things other than economic activity and material acquisition, for these are the indicators of being chosen. Wealthiness is next to godliness.

[5] Raymond Aron, *Main Currents in Sociological Thought,* Vol. II (New York: Basic Books, Inc., Publishers, 1967).

ideological base for the philosophical schools of Humanism, Enlightenment, and Utilitarianism, which developed in the wake of the Reformation.[6] The demand that each person seek his own foundations for belief has the further consequence of a questioning attitude which puts all institutions under scrutiny. Pietism also leads to sectarianism, that is, many separate groups of believers whose sects are distinguished by highly distinct definitions of God and his worship. Durkheim implies that such individual belief, magnified by modern industrial work and living conditions, is the source of many social pathologies because it cuts men off from their brothers, socially and psychologically. He calls this phenomenon anomie.[7]

Asceticism   Raymond Aron describes asceticism as follows:

> Mystical contact with God is one of the possible answers to the problem of evil, one of the paths of redemption. Asceticism is another path, another mode of redemption. . . . Asceticism is itself characterized by two fundamental modalities, asceticism in the world and asceticism outside the world. The Protestant ethic is the perfect example of asceticism in the world: activity pushed beyond the ordinary norm not for the purpose of pleasure and enjoyment, but in fulfillment of one's early duty.[8]

Puritanism   In the context of an analysis of the effect of puritanism and pietism on the development of science, Robert Merton delineates the basic motifs of puritanism as one of the dimensions of the Protestant ethos.[9] Generally speaking, this dimension of the ethos implores the individual to "work for the greater glory of

[6] Joachim Wach, *Sociology of Religion* (Chicago: University of Chicago Press, 1944), pp. 29, 146, 235, 316.

[7] Aron, *op. cit.*, pp. 39–42.

[8] *Ibid.*, p. 273.

[9] Robert Merton, *Social Theory and Social Structure*, rev. ed. (Glencoe, Ill.: The Free Press, 1957), pp. 574–606. Adapted with permission of The Macmillan Company. Copyright © 1957 by The Free Press, a Corporation. Copyright © 1949 by The Free Press.

God" and to work with the idea in mind that the "good of the many is a good even to be held in mind." Responsibility for building the kingdom of God and being one's brother's keeper is implicit. And, says Merton, this demands "systematic, methodic labor and constant diligence to one's calling." One must curb his passions by rationality. The Protestant ethos reinforces the pietistic notion that one's faith must be questioned and rationally weighed. This aspect of the ethos has had great effect on the secularization of western man and has been an impetus to science because the study of nature enables not only the control of nature technologically but also a fuller appreciation of God's works. This leads us to "admire the power, wisdom, and goodness of God manifested in his creation." At least, such was the interface between religion and science in the seventeenth century.

The Product of the Religious Enterprise   Raymond Aron, summarizing Durkheim's definition of religious activity, provides us again with a note on the present concern. Durkheim indicates that a product of this system is that it is at once more general than the reinforcement of the system-wide ideology and more theoretically subtle.

> What constitutes the category of the religious is the bipartite division of the world into what is profane and what is sacred. The sacred consists of a body of things, beliefs, and rites. When a number of sacred things (public objects which symbolize the shared focus and concerns of the society) maintain relations of coordination and subordination with one another so as to form a system of the same kind, this body of corresponding beliefs and rites constitutes a religion. Religion hence presupposes the sacred; next, the organization of beliefs regarding the sacred into a group; finally, rites or practices which proceed in a more or less logical manner from the body of beliefs.[10]

> Religion is too permanent, too profound an experience

---

[10] Aron, *op. cit.*, p. 48.

not to correspond to a true reality; and if this true reality is not God, then it must be the reality, so to speak, immediately below God, namely, society.[11]

There is also the implication in Durkheim's work that profane objects are generally objects of personal utility, objects of individual concern, or objects not conducive to, or related to, the solidarity of the group. Therefore, if we accept these premises about the nature of the religious we will find Durkheim's conclusion reasonable: that sacred objects are the embodiment of the collective focus of attention and their worship is the celebration of cooperative effort for the survival of the group (tribe or nation), the consequence of which is the survival of the individual. We can readily see Durkheim's further conclusion that men have never worshipped anything but their own society.

One may raise the question, Is the Protestant ethos (and the secularism, individualism, and rationalism it inspired) the basis of anomie because it produces a situation that is no longer a celebration of social solidarity as was the case with earlier forms of religion? Or, Is the modern solidarity principle outside of the boundaries of the religious enterprise in that the worship of the society is just that, political chauvinism or the patriotic focus upon the symbols of our political units? As Aron further characterizes Durkheim's premise: "Society favors the rise of beliefs because individuals brought together living in communion with one another are able in the exaltations of festivals to create the divine."[12]

When the Soviets judge the works of Freud to be theoretically unsound, is this greatly different from the Holy Office judging the works of Copernicus as heretical? For your own interest, note for a moment the fervor of the organization man as depicted by Whyte, think of the festival of political conventions, reflect upon the happening at Woodstock, May Day in Moscow, and Der Führer's mass meetings and book burnings, and a legion of other examples generally relegated to the realm of collective behavior in sociological textbooks. They are all very distinct examples in

---

[11] *Ibid.*, p. 58.
[12] *Ibid.*, p. 58.

terms of their properties and symbols, but all very alike in the celebration of collective will.

Interface with the Economic Enterprise   Probably the most well-known and generally accepted work on religion and economics is Max Weber's *The Protestant Ethic and the Spirit of Capitalism*. As Irving Zeitlin points out, this work "is to clarify the part that religious forces have played in forming the developing web of specifically worldly modern culture in the complex interaction of innumerable different historical factors."[13] In short, it is a work which seeks to aid in answering the question, "How do ideas become forces in history?" Weber, of course, recognized that as the economic system developed, it brought about change within the religious enterprise. However, it is mainly the effects of the religious ethic upon economic action which gets his attention in this treatise. Weber shows demographically how Protestants have historically revealed a tendency to develop economic modes of a particular nature—capitalism in particular. This tendency was not observed to the same extent among Catholics, even in similar geographic and political situations.

Weber's explanation of the difference between Protestants and Catholics (similar to Durkheim's explanation regarding suicide rates) is centered on the discussion of the character of their respective religious beliefs and practices. He found that pietism, puritanism, and asceticism and their characteristic demands for efficiency and personal excellence in the area of spiritual redemption force their counterpart in economic activity. This results in economic activity based on the directives of individual striving for acquisition of material goods, utilizing rational methodical techniques. Worldly success was the indicator of grace, and an indication that one had fulfilled the task of his calling. A man's worth, even in this day of supposed agnosticism, is still related to his assets or earning potential.

Interface with Science   In Merton's study of "Puritanism, Pietism and Science" the same kind of Weberian notion is generally put

---

[13] Zeitlin, *op. cit.*, p. 122.

forth to explain the rise of the natural sciences and the scientific mentality developing in the sixteenth and seventeenth centuries, and the continued prevalence of this concern in modern society.

It is the thesis of this study that the Puritan ethic, as an ideal typical expression of the value attitudes basic to ascetic Protestantism generally, so canalized the interests of the seventeenth century enlightenment as to constitute an important element in the enhanced cultivation of science.[14]

In other words, the implications involved in pietism and puritanism fostered the rational and empirical study of nature for the glorification of God, in keeping with the personal calling of the individual investigator.

Interface with the Political Enterprise   Philip Slater, in the June, 1970 edition of *Psychology Today,* provides an introduction to the following remarks in a most interesting way. In the context of a discussion concerning the conflicts between the culture of the older generation and that of the younger generation he evaluates the principle of scarcity in economic gratification and links it to politics in this way:

> Another logical consequence of scarcity assumptions is structured inequality. If there is not enough to go around even those who have more will find ways to prolong their advantage, and even *legitimate* it through various devices. The law itself, though philosophically committed to equality, is fundamentally a social device for maintaining structured systems of inequality (defining as crimes, for example, only those forms of theft and violence in which lower class persons engage). One of the major thrusts of the new culture, on the other hand, is equality. . . .[15] [italics added]

---

[14] Merton, *op. cit.,* p. 574.

[15] Philip Elliot Slater, *The Pursuit of Loneliness: American Culture at the Breaking Point* (Boston: Beacon Press, 1970), Chapter 5. The article reprinted in *Psychology Today* (June, 1970), p. 32, is entitled, "Cultures in Collision."

As this author has indicated in earlier parts of the text, the religious enterprise offers the foundations of the political ideology as a rationale for the political insulation and protection of a given economic system. A particular legal-political system will be designed to be consistent with the interests of those who are in a situation of being materially successful. Likewise, those who are materially successful will be in a position of being powerful enough to enact governmental structures which support their interests and ensure the maintenance of the economic mode. Also, if the governmental structure is to be deemed legitimate by the total population, the collective belief system will be consistent with the political ideology (whether the economic mode is fortunate in consequences for the majority or not). One can, therefore, appreciate how pietism and puritanism, as vague dimensions of a general Protestant belief system, reinforce the political-economic attitudes which prevail concerning private property, an honest day's work, and a requisite faith in the mysterious workings of the stock exchange.

Two criminologists, Marshall Clinard and Richard Quinney, recently reiterated this relationship in their discussion of the political nature of criminal law. They show the politico-economic aspects of criminal law by noting:

1. Specific rules of conduct are created by a recognized authority.
2. Designated officials interpret and enforce these rules.
3. The code is binding on all persons within a given political unit.[16]

They go on to note how a decision as to who is the criminal is made in the enforcement and interpretation of the criminal law. In this way the value-attitudes and activities of groups having relative amounts of power within the system can and do enter into the establishment of the criminality of an individual or group. And the religious establishment, one might add, is in the position of having to rationalize and legitimate this action. There is probably more

---

[16] Marshall Clinard, and Richard Quinney, *Criminal Behavior Systems* (New York: Holt, Rinehart and Winston, 1967), pp. 177–178.

than meets the eye in the symbolic walking of the last mile by the priest and the condemned, or, for that matter, in the convocation given by the chaplain at the beginning of a congressional session. In the following chapters, which deal with the systems of science, politics, and economics, the role of the religious enterprise will become more observable. As we get into the analysis of these other systems, it will be noted how the historical occurrences of religious reformation, capitalization, fundamental democratization, scientific revolution, industrialization, and intellectual enlightenment were mutually reinforcing system interactions.

Reformation, which made critique of the sacred institutions a possibility, could be seen as opening the door of intellectual scrutiny that made possible the critical analysis of all man's institutional modes of acting and thinking. Such a critical mentality was essential to laying a cultural foundation for the building of new economic, scientific, and political structures that grew rapidly in western culture from the sixteenth century on, each giving structural reinforcement to the other.

This is not to say that the Catholic monolith of the medieval world did not play a part in this transition. It was Catholic scholarship that introduced the rediscovery of Greek sophistry and Roman jurisprudence which brought the Renaissance to Europe, thus having the effect of launching the Reformation, the Age of Reason, and artistic and economic innovation.

However, from that time the laws of the political institution reflected more and more the priorities of a Protestant world and a capitalist economic mode. The medieval Catholic laws against usury were replaced by laws protecting private property and the prerogative of the entrepreneur as intellectual notions of individualism and economic modes of capitalization grew in importance. Church definitions of sin and falling from grace were replaced by state definitions of crime, breach of contract, or the establishment of economic liability. Divine right of kings was replaced by the constitutional rights of parliaments, and nationalism and patriotism replaced the fervor of religious crusades.

Chapter 13 The Enterprise of Science

Incipient and actual attacks upon the integrity of science have led scientists to recognize their dependence on particular types of social structure.

Since [the above] was written in 1942, it is evident that the explosion at Hiroshima has jarred many more scientists into an awareness of the social consequences of their works.[1]

In the above quotations the kernel of Merton's description concerning the mutual dependence of science and social order provides a most succinct introduction to the sociology of science. Many writers have dealt with the impact of science and creativity and invention and technology upon society in recent years, but

---

[1] Robert K. Merton, "Science and Democratic Institutions," in *Social Theory and Social Structure,* rev. ed. (Glencoe, Ill.: The Free Press, 1957), p. 550.

Merton reinforced the idea that both sides of the coin must be considered.[2] The historical studies of A. C. Crombie (*Medieval and Early Modern Science*)[3] and Herbert Butterfield (*The Origins of Modern Science*)[4] imply strongly enough the conservative effects of medieval theocracy upon scientific investigation, discovery and implementation, but it is in the sociological analysis of Merton that the most satisfying assessment of the relationship between science and the other sectors of society is found.

This chapter deals with both concerns. It is based primarily on definitions and theoretical dimensions provided by Merton,[5] Storer,[6] and Barber[7] for its structure. However, it is a fairly free interpretation of these persons' works designed for the introductory reader. The general purpose is to illustrate how science itself might be the subject of investigation and the role this enterprise plays within the broader spectrum of the social macrocosm.

Boundaries of the System   As was indicated above, the boundaries of a system can be practically defined by a notation of the norms particular to that system and its goals and products. If we begin with the assumption that a scientist is one who seeks to perfect and utilize the art of obtaining accurate and certified knowledge about phenomena which he deems interesting or important, and if we accept Merton's assumption that the goals of a social system dictate its norms, we can easily accept Merton's inventory of basic norms which mark the boundaries of the ethos of the scientific community.

If we accept the premise that the goal of this system is the extension of certified knowledge, then it follows that certain

---

[2] *Ibid.*

[3] Alistair C. Crombie, *Medieval and Early Modern Science,* Vols. I and II (Cambridge: Harvard University Press, 1961).

[4] Herbert Butterfield, *The Origins of Modern Science: 1300–1800,* rev. ed. (New York: Macmillan, 1959).

[5] Merton, *op. cit.*

[6] Norman Storer, *The Social System of Science* (New York: Holt, Rinehart and Winston, 1966).

[7] Bernard Barber, *Science and the Social Order* (New York: Collier Books, 1962).

technical norms for acquiring and verifying this knowledge will control the behavior of the actors in the system. Such technical norms are stated quite explicitly in the opening chapter of almost any text for an introductory college course in a scientific discipline. If knowledge is to be certified, that is, if it is to be acceptable as an accumulation of true statements about observable facts, it must be gathered and verified according to technical modes general to the system of behaving actors. According to most texts in methods or philosophy of science, the technical norms of the scientific enterprise fall into two categories:

1. *Empirical:* Established techniques for observation, measurement, and verification (techniques of induction).
2. *Logical:* Established techniques for maintaining consistency of meaning, validity of statements, and extension of this knowledge to further hypothesize about relationships yet unverified (deductive techniques).

In order to insure adherence to the technical norms by all members of the scientific community, some system-wide imperatives must exist. Assurance that the technical norms will be enforced means that collective goals can be realized. These system-wide imperatives, or general ethos of the community, form the boundary of the system of science. Merton has listed four general imperatives which characterize this system:

1. Universalism.
2. Communism or communality.
3. Disinterestedness.
4. Organized skepticism.[8]

Bernard Barber adds rationality and emotional neutrality to the list.[9] It appears to this writer, however, that adherence to the norms of rationality and emotional neutrality are subsumed under Merton's four categories. Therefore, the four imperatives of Merton will be utilized for the present sketch of the ethos of the scientific enterprise.

---

[8] Merton, *op. cit.,* pp. 553–560.
[9] Barber, *op. cit.,* pp. 122–142.

As in any system actors deviate from the norms. Likewise, as in any system, deviations and resulting sanctions give evidence to the existence of the imperatives and reinforce them within the system. One can see that the imperatives might engender negative feedback when the system interacts with other systems, because these imperatives sometimes contradict the imperatives of the systems of religion, economics, or politics. This conflict will become more apparent as we discuss this question further.

Universalism   Universalism simply refers to the imperative that objects should be referred to by the use of general system-wide standards instead of by the particularistic or personal standards of an individual actor. Such an imperative also suggests objectivity and a certain emotional neutrality toward the objects of study. In other words, one should not allow his personal likes and dislikes to interfere with objective observation and description of the phenomena being studied. In system interface with other systems in society, this imperative means that religious, economic, and political priorities should not be utilized in the scientific discourse relating to the phenomena being studied. For example, one may have a personal dislike for reptiles, but as a zoologist he should not refer to them as "slimy little snakes" or as the "embodiment of the devil," or seek to prove in his research that snakes lost their legs when they incurred the wrath of God.

In addition, universalism refers to the technical notion that laws of nature apply universally. Hydrogen and oxygen under specified conditions always combine to form water as long as hydrogen and oxygen and water are universally defined and semantically treated the same way. This implies not only universal standards for operations but also universal language in the scientific community.

Therefore, an actor should only be excluded from the system if he exhibits incompetence in his work. He should not be excluded because of personal characteristics which have no bearing on his ability to carry out the technical norms and system imperatives in a competent fashion. This notion derives from the expertise dimension of rational organization discussed in the chapter on bureaucracy.

Communism or Communality   This imperative refers to the common ownership of certain "products" within the system. In this case, the products would be ideas, scientific principles, or the certified knowledge that was mentioned above. For example, Newton had no property claims on the laws of gravitation as scientific principles. The imperative implies that one's scientific research should be motivated by making a contribution to the discipline rather than by personal aggrandizement or the accumulation of personal wealth or power. The scientific tradition is considered a common heritage. Merton indicates that the only claim one can ethically make for a discovery is for recognition. When a discovery has a name of a scientist attached to it (Boyle's Law, Einstein's Theory), this practice is both a commemoration and a technique for cataloging the discovery. This imperative also implies that the scientist will maintain a stance of humility affirming that he could not have made the discovery without the work of previous scientists.

When the scientific enterprise is in interface with other systems, problems do occur at this point. What happens to scientists whose ideas are implemented in the economic sphere? In such cases, patents protect the legal owners of ideas; this appears to be somewhat contradictory to the imperative of communality. Also, there is the possibility of sanctions within the system for plagiarism, or the utilization of someone's principle without due credit. Embodied in this imperative is the notion that research findings are commonly owned by all of the actors in the system. However, in interface with economic imperatives it is not uncommon for fees to be paid to journals and publishing houses for permission to use a graph or quotation which has been copyrighted.

Disinterestedness   Closely related to communality, this imperative, as both Merton and Storer see it, prohibits the scientist from making personal recognition the major goal of his work. The scientist is assumed to be involved in the acquisition of knowledge for its own sake. This type of system-wide control has the effect of defining the scientist's role behavior. There are rather severe penalties for fraud and quackery within the scientific system. This also brings weight to bear on the political-legal system to control actors outside of the system who use the image of science to defraud the public. Some forms of deviation are more subtle than fraud; for example, a particular scientist may be racing for a Nobel prize, and he may try to improve his chances by withholding information from others working on the same problem. In such cases, sanctions may vary from a judgment of bad taste and censure to actual expulsion from the community of scholars.

Merton indicates that a greater possibility for chicanery exists with the service professions, that is, among those who implement scientific knowledge for the public. These people are more peripheral to the controls of the system. He also notes how "the borrowed authority of science bestows prestige on unscientific discoveries,"[10] a behavior this writer quite regularly observes in advertising. A case in point would be the use of an actor defined by the public as an M.D. because of his usual role on TV, giving testimony to the wondrous effects of a certain brand of aspirin.

Organized Skepticism   This imperative seeks to foster the suspension of judgments and the suspension of practical implementation of discoveries until all of the facts are in. Likewise, it makes each scientist responsible for the validity of his work. If a scientist finds that the work of his colleagues is not valid, he is obligated to make this known to others in the system. In addition, his motive for doing so should be to foster the acquisition of true knowledge and not the sweet satisfaction of finding his colleague in error, nor the retribution of "sour grapes" by having been "scooped" by his colleagues. The scientist must always maintain a certain doubt about his own work. What is a vice in the religious ethic is in this case a virtue. Scientific principles or theories must not be given the status of dogma or the weight of eternal truth. In interface with other systems this can be problematic because economic and political decision makers are sometimes impatient to put the principle to work in some practical fashion.

The Interface with the Other Systems   The problem of interaction between systems will become more apparent in subsequent

---

[10] Merton, *op. cit.*, p. 559.

chapters as all the systems eventually are defined; however, an example of actors involved in the discovery process will illuminate some of the possible junctures at which feedback takes place. The example to be used is the narrative of the discovery of the structure of the DNA molecule supplied by James Watson's best-selling book, *The Double Helix*.[11] Here we have an account by one of the people involved in a major scientific discovery which sheds some light on the multiplicity of complex motives and actions which took place. It is also a tacit confession of the deviations from the imperatives of the system and hence a reinforcement of them.

In 1962 James Watson and Francis Crick were awarded the Nobel prize for their work defining the structure of the DNA molecule. This was the culmination of activities which took place between the years 1951 and 1953. The story, told by Watson, is an interesting and exciting narrative, a drama as intriguing and full of human emotion as Irving Wallace's fictionalized account of a similar theme in *The Prize*. Affection, hostility, intrigue, politics, and competition fill the pages of this book, but it is not fiction and it is not about 007. It is about those disinterested and skeptical searchers of truth who were just being discussed—the actors in the system of science. Beyond the description of the human dimension of the laboratory, the book also offers a very good account of the techniques of induction and deduction which are manifestly or latently involved in the process of discovery.

Watson was a postdoctoral student working only tenuously within the bounds of the restrictions of his fellowship (the stipend ostensibly defined Denmark as the place of study) at Cavendish Laboratory in England. Crick, according to the account, was a walking encyclopedia whose main contribution at Cavendish was that of a source of information and instant conversation, having contributed nothing substantive since his research during World War II. He was a man of great imagination possessing a germinal mind. The accident of Watson and Crick coming together and sharing their interest and hypotheses about molecular structures

---

[11] James Watson, *The Double Helix* (New York: Atheneum, 1968).

in the class of the DNA molecule turned out to be quite advantageous.

They both possessed parts of the conceptual jigsaw. When they put them together the whole picture was not yet complete, but it was enough to convince them that they were on the right track. To complete the picture they needed more parts of the puzzle. Who possessed these parts? How could they get them without giving their part of the puzzle to these other investigators who might then beat them to the solution? That is the story.

They required the knowledge of Linus Pauling, whose expertise was in the area of information concerning the ways in which parts of molecules are structurally bonded together. A great deal of this Pauling had already made available in a textbook (communality); however, Watson found it necessary to study chemistry in order to decipher this. He had been advised against an academic program in chemistry after a rather serious explosion had occurred during an experiment in his undergraduate days. On top of that, his fellowship was not granted for the purpose of studying chemistry, and the administrator of the grant could cut him off at any time. Thus, he had to work on the DNA problem rather secretively. Crick was also advised during the process to get off the DNA project and get back to work on what Professor Bragg, the administrator of Cavendish Laboratory, felt would be a more profitable expenditure of energy and talent. Therefore, Crick also had to work on this problem only as an avocation—to all appearances at least.

Crick and Watson also required the assistance of Rosalind Franklin, an expert in X-ray microscopy, for basic inductive observations to bring further clues to bear on Watson's hypothesis that the structure was helical and clues as to how many helices were involved. They did not have the time or training to duplicate these techniques themselves, at least as well as Miss Franklin had mastered them. Meanwhile, she was having problems with Maurice Wilkins (or he with her) relative to male dominance in his lab at Kings College, and she was exhibiting a certain hostility toward male scientists in general as a feminist reaction to their chauvinism. This meant that she would give little attention or judgment of plausibility to Watson and Crick's hypothesis or attend to their pressing need for clear X-ray diffraction pictures. Mr. Wilkins seemed interested (he also received Nobel recognition in 1962) but did not want to incur the wrath of Rosalind and further upset the balance of relative interpersonal peace in his laboratory. Further, Crick and Watson were not able to obtain a chit from Bragg to get materials from the lab workshop for constructing the model of the molecule. They worked with bits of wire, cardboard, and whatever they could find to rough in the model as they theorized its structure to be.

Bit by bit they proceeded closer and closer to the answer. Solving the puzzle was in sight except for a few critical parts. Then they received the news that Pauling would visit the lab. They were sure that he would ask to see Rosalind's pictures when he visited Wilkin's lab and that he would ask to see the developing gerry-built model when he visited Cavendish. They figured that this was all he needed to solve the puzzle himself. Then they had a stroke of luck. Pauling was detained at the airport and sent home for security reasons by U.S. Government officials. This was the era of McCarthyism and it seems that Pauling's loyalties were in question because of his pronouncements in favor of peaceful coexistence (interface with politics).

Shortly thereafter, Pauling published an article in which he produced what he thought was the structure of the DNA molecule. Crick and Watson were relieved to find that he had made a mistake in his model. They reasoned that if his mistake could be kept a secret they would have at least six weeks to complete their project and still beat him to the punch. Withholding this information was difficult because Crick was corresponding with Max Delbruck, a colleague of Pauling's, for assistance and critical comment on his developing theory. Also, Pauling's son was in residence at Cavendish as a graduate assistant and in constant contact with Crick and Watson. Watson finally picked up enough of the basics of the X-ray diffraction technique to get a pretty clear diffraction film of the molecule structure to assure himself that the elements were arranged in a double helix structure. Crick and Watson were then able to acquire confirmation from Wilkins and Franklin at this point. Once they had this confirmation, Sir Bragg, who now saw the possibility of his laboratory scooping Cal Tech on the DNA problem, gave them the go-ahead. The model was built, the article describing it was written (with all humility and disinterestedness), and the Nobel prize was in the bag.

One might imagine that similar stories could be written by Jonas Salk regarding the discovery of the polio vaccine, by Dr. Barnard regarding his race with Dr. Shumway for the first human heart transplant, and by the men of the Manhattan project who perfected the atomic bomb. All of these stories would portray a situation that strays a bit from the exposition of the scientific method that students put to memory as if it were a catechism.

This brief resumé of Watson's story illustrates the way in which the basic motivation systems of the individual are channeled and modified by the ethos or normative structure within which the individual lives and works. It also indicates that the system ethics of science are not 100 per cent efficient nor would we want them to be. It is entirely possible that without the very human motivation for psychological rewards and self-aggrandizement flexibly controlled by the ethic of communality there would not be sufficient impetus to spark the discovery process. The story also illustrates the more subtle effects of institutionalized skepticism. For whatever her reasons, had Miss Franklin not exhibited the skepticism and reserve that she did toward Watson's and Crick's scheme, they might not have been moved to employ corrective reevaluation of the hypothesis until the parts fitted perfectly.

Interface with Religion   In the preceding chapter there was a discussion of the religious ethos and its effect upon the development of the scientific mentality and the developing scientific enterprise and its technological offspring. At this point, the effect of the scientific enterprise upon the system of religion is of concern. Such a concern is sometimes phrased as the effect of science and technology upon the moral order.

Daniel Bell has described the nature of this interaction in *The End of Ideology*.[12] Pitirim Sorokin addresses the same problem in *The Crisis of Our Age*.[13] Alvin Gouldner and Richard Peterson pinpoint some of the finer processes in this interaction in *Notes*

[12] Daniel Bell, *The End of Ideology* (Glencoe, Ill.: The Free Press, 1960).
[13] Pitirim Sorokin, *The Crisis of Our Age* (New York: E. P. Dutton, 1941).

on Technology and the Moral Order.[14] Karl Mannheim discusses this somewhat less directly in *Ideology and Utopia.*[15] And post-scripts for the decade of the sixties are found in Victor Ferkiss's *Technological Man*[16] and Theodore Roszak's *The Making of a Counter Culture.*[17]

The literature provides a general sketch of the interface that might be summarized in this manner: In its skirmishes with the enterprise of science, religion has won some battles, but in the long run, is losing the war. It appears that once the scientific mentality, conceived in Catholic scholasticism and sustained in the womb of the Protestant Reformation, began to grow and prosper in western culture, its definition of reality and its criteria for truth became more and more pervasive.

To counteract what was perceived as a threat to the cosmology of the religious enterprise, religionists sought to justify their existence and the existence of their ideals by the use of scientific criteria. The result of this action (attempts to prove the existence of God and *the priority* of belief empirically or logically) was unfortunate for the religious system. Religionists failed to realize that belief systems have to be justified on grounds different from scientific knowledge about the phenomenal world. For instance, the establishment of the date of creation empirically by biblical research brought religious cosmology and ideology into the laboratory of geology and astronomy, and the kind of scrutiny it received there lent nothing to its credibility.

Seeking to remove the threat of the negative feedback which resulted from this interface by joining with the system of science only weakened the position of the religious enterprise. Had western religion taken the advice of its major prophet and rendered unto Caesar that which was Caesar's and unto God that which was God's, a distinct role for the religious establishment

[14] Alvin Gouldner, and Richard Peterson, *Notes on Technology and the Moral Order* (Indianapolis, Ind.: Bobbs-Merrill, 1962).

[15] Karl Mannheim, *Ideology and Utopia* (New York: Harcourt, Brace and World, 1936).

[16] Victor Ferkiss, *Technological Man* (New York: New American Library, 1969).

[17] Theodore Roszak, *The Making of a Counter Culture* (New York: Doubleday, 1969).

might have evolved—a role which science could not have played and never will play—a system which offers a definition of meaning for existence and an ideological focus for social solidarity. When the scientific enterprise is asked to play this role, it fails. Thus by the end of the nineteenth century the result was a weakened religious system that could offer little to man as he entered the modern hyper-industrial age. The ideology gap left by a secular religion could not be filled by nihilistic existential philosophy, nor could it be filled by the ideology created by attempts of technologists, economists, or politicians. Such was the crisis of western society. Sorokin called it the Sensate Age—the age in which man sought truth and meaning utilizing only that which the senses can perceive. There were no great beliefs that could hold man's mind and give him courage. There were only temporary visions of political and economic utopias which, lacking the justification of widespread belief, sought the justification of force.

Technological, political, and economic expertise could not forestall the bloodbaths and the sterility of soul which marked the early portion of the twentieth century. Likewise, it is generally recognized that it required well-trained technicians, efficient administrators, and effective logicians to perform the genocide ·and attempted genocide of western man's recent history. There is now the recognition that science can tell us how, but it cannot tell us why.

Interface with the Systems of Economics and Politics   Generally speaking, the interaction between the system of science-technology and those of the economic and political enterprises produces more positive than negative feedback. That is not to say that the relationship is completely a happy one, but economic and political impositions upon the scientific system are, in most cases, short-lived. There are two possible explanations for this: (1) Even in this day, there are certain imputations of mystique attached to the producers of scientific "wonders." Lay society is often impressed by the creations of the scientific community in much the same way as primitives are impressed and held in awe by the sleight-of-hand of the local shaman. (2) It is quite obvious that the political and economic sectors of the total social system are ready consumers of the commodities produced by the scientific enterprise—and they pay dearly for these commodities. However, if they require what only the scientist can offer they will see to it that the scientist has the necessary economic and political insulation prerequisite to his work.

On the other hand, activities within the scientific community not in line with the short-term priorities of economic or political interests will either be ignored or reacted to in a negative fashion. Scientists can quickly lose the aura of society's darlings should they embark on paths that conflict with the interests of political or economic policy makers. Likewise, it is also possible that scientists adhering to the ethos of the system of science will find themselves in a position of being adjudged deviant in relation to the existing political ethos. In the act of adhering to the principle of communality one may share the fruits of scientific discovery with a colleague in another political system and thus find himself legally defined as a traitor (if in fact the practical applications of the discovery are appreciated by lay society or political figures).

In other situations scientists and technologists may become unwitting tools of existing political policy makers.[18] Political systems might even compete for the loyalties of certain members of the scientific community whose work they perceive as important to their priorities being realized.

More subtle aspects of this interface also occur. It was noted earlier that when systems are in interface a system may take on some of the dimensions of a more dominant system so as to protect its own existence when a threat is perceived. Such is the case when, for instance, institutions of research or learning will, over time, acquire the administrative operational structures of economic organizations and seek to apply modes of action which have proven profitable in industrial settings to educational or research settings. This probably occurs because education itself is one of the focuses of the interface. Generally speaking, educational institutions are the shared properties of the four basic systems. This is the source of recruitment of members for all

---

[18] See comments on Project Camelot, in *Ethics, Politics and Social Research*, Gideon Sjoberg (Cambridge, Mass.: Schenkman Publishing, 1967), pp. 141–161.

systems and generally they share in the cost and administration of these processes. However, cost-price theory and rationalized administration, although proven as advantageous in the economic sector or governmental sector of a society, usually have less fortunate consequences when applied to the daily activities of a university or college system or in the research laboratory.

The ultimate application of this attempt to alleviate negative feedback in system interface is to place individuals with proven executive competence in business or the military in executive administrative positions in the university or in the laboratory. Industrial productivity and excellence in scholarship, research creativity, and teaching are very different things.

Chapter 14

The Enterprise of Economics: The Production and Distribution of Wealth

"Speak out and tell me frankly what the profits have been, what they are now, and what our financial condition is. It's impossible, you know, to go on like this in the dark."[1]

The final problem of the productive society is what it produces. This manifests itself in an implacable tendency to provide an opulent supply of some things and a niggardly supply of others. This disparity carries to the point where it is a cause of social discomfort and social unhealth.[2]

[1] Ann Dunnigan, ed. and trans., *Anton Chekhov, Selected Stories* (New York: New American Library, 1960), p. 219. The quotation is taken from the short story, "Three Years," first published in 1895.

[2] Kenneth Galbraith, "The Affluent Society," in *Man in Contemporary Society*, ed. William Taber (New York: Columbia University Press, 1962), p. 906.

To begin this description of the economic system, the author would reiterate that a description of a system is difficult indeed unless there is a shared assumption that no system is a static thing. Like other systems, the economic system is a fluid and ever-changing phenomenon. The legal codes of a society which maintain the economic order only establish its character for a time. Thus the description begins with the assumption that the economic system characteristic of the industrial west is an evolutionary process most generally referred to as capitalism.

The term capitalism has been greatly overused and its meaning has become fogged. Therefore, the attempt to describe this systemic enterprise must also involve the definition of a rather vague term which has acquired emotional connotations unbecoming to a scientific term. Such clarification could preclude many debates about modern problems which have had minimal usefulness, for they are debates over semantics rather than about realities. The leftist who cries out against the evils of capitalism is more than likely decrying the nature of the octopus-like corporate bureaucracy of a monopoly that through benign neglect or supposed avarice condemns men to slave-like existences. The local patriot who enjoins us to save the free enterprise system is most probably hoping to ensure the continued existence of the small entrepreneur —the local greengrocer, the barber, or the clothier.

Their argument gets nowhere because they have no common definitions. They are likewise talking of different things at different levels of abstraction. They are talking about realities experienced by both and they are expressing implied ideals (which may not be contradictory) and their fervor results, no doubt, from a realization that perhaps their ideals are being violated.

But that is as far as it goes. What is capitalism? What is the ethos that drives it? Where has it come from? Where is it going? What is its relation to other modern enterprises in interface?

It appears from a cursory review of literature dealing with western economic activity that the technical requirements for the existence of this particular type of system, a privately incorporated economy, are the following:

1.   The institutionalized norm of private property.

2. The existence of a free market.
3. A supply of labor free to accept or reject employment.
4. The availability of technological specialists and the application of their genius to production.

These requirements will be defined in the context of the exposition of the capitalization process later. For now, let us continue with the basic assumptions.

The next set of assumptions, again prevalent in the literature, deal with the dimensions of the economic ethos which provide the ideological reinforcement for an environment conducive to meeting the requirements and the maintenance of such a system. These are briefly:

1. The ethic of workmanship.
2. The ethic of utilitarianism and efficiency which also includes the ethic of a critical mentality—a negative attitude toward tradition and a positive appeal to progress and innovation.
3. The ethic of acquisitiveness and profit.
4. The ethic of distributive justice.

The next set of assumptions is that set concerned with the products of the system. The output of the capitalist system is a particular mode of producing commodities (goods and wealth) and a particular mode of distributing these goods and wealth throughout the society of system actors. Briefly:

1. The cost of production is determined by the relative efficiency of production technology and recorded by cost accounting.
2. The price of products is determined by cost and profit definitions and then by supply and demand relations.
3. Market relations are carried out by a money standard.

At this point a look at some prevalent definitions of capitalism from the sociological point of view may aid in the clarification of the concepts and terms introduced above, before the process of capitalization is further described. Don Martindale in *Institutions,*

Organizations, and Mass Society[3] reviews the work of several commentators on this topic and provides additional information for defining the concepts. Joseph Schumpeter's idea is that a society's economic system is capitalistic if it entrusts all of its economic activities to private businessmen.[4] Involved in this are the concomitant social conditions of:

1. Private ownership of nonpersonal means of production (land, mines, industrial plants, and equipment).
2. Production activities carried on for the purposes of acquisition of private profit.
3. The existence of the institution of bank credit.

From the work of Harry Elmer Barnes, Martindale gleans these attitudes and actions regarding capitalism:[5]

1. There is a desire for private profit.
2. The estimation of social status is in terms of monetary wealth.
3. The value of goods and services is established by market-determined prices.
4. There is an accumulation of monetary rewards for investment.
5. There exists a free (uninhibited and nonrestricted) market.
6. There exists a supply of labor free to move from one job to another.
7. There exists a credit system adequate to economic means of the entrepreneur.

All in all, the purpose of such a system is to gain private profit by means of free competition and a driving spirit of private initiative.

Finally, from the work of Max Weber, Martindale notes several key concepts as regard capitalism.[6] According to Weber,

---

[3] Don Martindale, *Institutions, Organizations, and Mass Society* (Boston: Houghton Mifflin, 1966).

[4] *Ibid.*, p. 210.

[5] *Ibid.*

[6] *Ibid.*, p. 211.

the definitive aspect of capitalism is the system-wide use of accounting. One can appreciate Weber's use of accounting as the indicator of a capitalistic society because it assumes the existence of a monetary standard and the motive of profit maximization. Martindale lists the following distinctions found in the work of Weber:

1. Freedom in the market place.
2. The utilization of rationalism and technology.
3. The existence of calculable law—precise codes and statutes which deal with commerce and contract.
4. Free labor.
5. The commercialization of economic life.

This adds nothing to the original definition, but it does enlarge upon the concepts and assumptions with which the discussion of capitalism must begin. Moreover, these listings of distinctions and dimensions are static descriptions of an economic system. And, insofar as this is true they present a somewhat misleading picture.

If we were to look at capitalization as a dynamic systemic process, we would probably find that the various items as listed are properties of capitalism, although they may not always exist in all its stages of development. For it is probably safe to say that most characterizations of capitalism are static pictures of some past stage in this process (the near past at that). They are pictures of nineteenth century economic realities. As such, they tell us nothing of the early stages of the process, nor of the present modifications, nor of tomorrow's possibilities. When we look at the process of capitalization, we see it as a development in western experience inextricably tied to religious, intellectual, moral, and demographic developments, and none of these processes can be fully understood without some appreciable understanding of all. Therefore, we must approach the assessment of the economic system in terms of other activity which is not always strictly economic.

Most literature of this more historically inclusive scope and sociological insight attempts to afford this understanding. One kind of developmental theory consistent with this notion might be diagrammed as the following, and it might span time from the eighth to the nineteenth century.

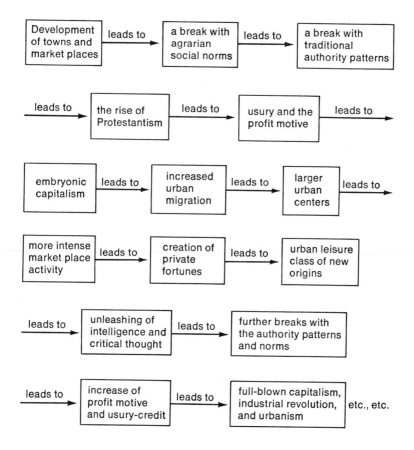

A close look at one such developmental theory will perhaps provide clarification of the conceptualization of the capitalization process. The description that follows is from such an analysis which is found in an article by Henri Pirenne, "Stages in the Social History of Capitalism."[7]

It is Pirenne's purpose to characterize the nature of capitalism for each epoch of western history and to search for the origin of capitalist man. It is Pirenne's claim that capitalists are not of

[7] Henri Pirenne, "Stages in the Social History of Capitalism," in *Class, Status, and Power,* ed. Reinhard Bendix, and Seymour Martin Lipset (Glencoe, Ill.: The Free Press, 1953), pp. 97–107.

a continuous type in history; rather, there is a new capitalist at each turning point in history. Explicit in his analysis is the notion that the capitalist is bold, courageous, and enterprising by definition, and he is one who breaks with the confines of the established order. However, those types who are innovative at the beginning of an epoch are precisely the ones who are highly normative and conservative at the close of an epoch. And, as one kind of capitalist becomes passive in an order conducive to his will, he is replaced by a new enterprising type. Pirenne's conclusion is that there are as many types of capitalists as there are major epochs in western history.

To begin with, Pirenne identifies what he considers to be the abstract essential features of capitalist behavior:

1. Individual enterprise.
2. Advances on credit.
3. Commercial profits.
4. Speculation.

He then goes on to note how these already existed (if they were not normatively acceptable) as early as the twelfth century in the city states of Venice, Genoa, Florence, Ghent, Bruges, Ypres, and Tournai. Moreover, there were anticipatory indications of these phenomena as early as the eighth century. Pirenne does not claim that the preponderant economic force was capitalism prior to the seventeenth century; rather, he only makes a case for the existence of conditions conducive to the capitalist mode early in western history. He notes that medieval Europe may have been anti-capitalistic but it was not a-capitalistic. The fact recorded in history that medieval mentality reacted against usury and vagabond merchants only indicates their existence. The church and the monarchies must have recognized that because they attempted to defend themselves against them. In its beginnings, the capitalist mode was a deviant and anti-establishment form.

Pirenne saw the beginnings of the germ of capitalist behavior observably existing in the pre-urban economic system of the nineteenth century, even though historical data are sketchy concerning this period. He made the assumption that the Roman system had all but disappeared in Europe by the eighth century and what had developed by the eleventh century was a system which was basically agricultural and feudal. Furthermore, he assumed that the production of the feudal farms was not of such an extent that a surplus would have been available for commercial export and marketplace trading. Any wealth which was accumulated by the landed aristocracy was from revenues received from peasants tilling the landholdings. However, there is evidence that some commercial traffic existed around commodities of which there may have been surpluses time and again on a sporadic basis. These commodities were probably wine, salt, and fabrics. The agents of the few exchanges which took place were called *negoziatóres, negociatores* or middlemen who worked for the lord or bishop finding buyers for surpluses when they occurred. Although little is known of them, Pirenne assumed that a bit of the capitalist spirit was to be found in these merchants who took advantage of opportunity. "They were men without a country ready to seize on any means of existence that came their way—pursuers of adventure, half trader, half pirate."[8] The spirit of enterprise was found in these men who were marginal to society and, therefore, unbound by its traditions; however, other essential features of capitalist men were not present, i.e., "violence of appetite took the place of calculation."[9]

In this period, only the possession of land or being indentured to a possessor of land could give one a normal social classification. Outside of that boundary were the "confused masses, beggars, mercenaries, bargemen, drovers, peddlers, and traders."[10] In time, however, these marginals of various occupations collected at the crossroads, river crossings, and seaports of Europe, establishing a collection of shacks and tents which were the nuclei of towns to come. There they plied their services, which were the beginning of trading occupations. Some *negociatores* accumulated wealth, built more stable accommodations, and the beginning of the walled city emerged. Little was known of capital, however, for money, the portable means of exchange, had not yet become

[8] *Ibid.*, p. 99.
[9] *Ibid.*
[10] *Ibid.*

prevalent. Therefore, accounting and speculation, which required the concept of capital, were not prevalent either. Fortunes accumulated in the form of jewelry, metals, and objects of art, and crafted goods; and these accumulated mostly in the church. Revenues were collected in kind by landowners but these were idle fortunes with no economic purpose. Wealth was fixed motionless in castle and cathedral.

The progress of economic activity continued at the intersections of frequent travel. By the twelfth century these towns had grown to more stable proportions. Within the walls were bishops, nuns, and clerics; outside the walls were fairs, the tents of merchants, and the wagons of peddlers and smiths. Generally, they dealt with the exchanges between local peasantry, but there were the merchant adventurers with exotic goods from far-off places looking to trade for local produce—"buying cheap and selling dear."

The activity increased to a point where the intensity of trade provided new means of existence other than tilling the soil. Peasants migrated to places of commerce to handle the merchandise, to tow boats and to find a regular occupation. In time, the idea and the hope of gain was aroused. Soon suburbs joined the walled city and what was once the nucleus of the city became the "priests' quarter," surrounded on all sides by lay life. Pirenne saw these migrants to the urban centers as the pioneers of commerce because they were marginal to a way of life which was becoming passé. They brought resources that built a commercial age—"The strength of their arms, the force of their wills, and the clearness of their intelligence."[11]

So, noted Pirenne, the ancestors of the bourgeoisie were found in these "wandering beings, who, having no land to cultivate floated across the surface of society, hiring themselves out, enlisting in the armies and building their fortunes in movable property."[12] With these new migrants are found the seeds of calculation and speculation.

There were certain things which stood as obstacles to their

[11] *Ibid.,* p. 101.
[12] *Ibid.*

endeavors—insecurity on the road and the imposition of revenues and tolls by the landed aristocracy. Therefore, the next phase brought merchants banded together in associations such as guilds, Hanse, caritates, and caravans to solve problems collectively. They moved in convoys from town to town buying and selling in common and dividing the profits. In so doing, they were wholesalers, leaving the retailing to the local peasantry. Their guild constitutions usually excluded retailers and craftsmen from their membership. To secure their way of life and means of existence they established trade regulations and regional monopolies. However, the only restrictions upon themselves were found in commerce itself, where force took the place of law. At that stage (twelfth to fifteenth centuries) the towns were still centers of trade rather than centers of industry, which left peasants in the outlying areas to sell their homemade wares to local merchants.

Soon the fortunes acquired in trade transformed the merchants into urban land proprietors. They became patricians and renters, and noted Pirenne, "The grandsons of commerce content themselves with living off the revenues and bid farewell to the chances of wandering life."[13] They became gentlemen and assumed control of municipal administration.

At this point, a new entrepreneur and adventurer migrated to the towns. These were craftsmen and artisans who established manufacturing combinations, or, in port towns, they were explorers and navigators. The port towns further developed international exportation. To do so it was necessary that a money standard be developed on an international scale. This development became possible because new sources of precious metals were found in the Americas. As the coining of money proceeded, the institution of banking developed with the concept of credit and interest on loans (still prohibited by the religious establishment), which became an essential characteristic of commerce. As the circulation of money expanded, it was regulated by merchant and monarch alike. The new capitalist, however, overcame restrictions by making loans to princes and monasteries whose fortunes were dwindling in the urban transition.

---

[13] *Ibid.*, p. 103.

This capitalist did not have the freedom of earlier times as the propertied descendants of the old capitalist controlled the towns and enforced protective regulations to maintain the security of their class. Tariffs on goods which competed with those manufactured locally were enacted. The levied taxes limited egress to the towns. As a result, certain types of manufacturing and trade became monopolies of particular towns. But, Pirenne noted, "intelligence is the instrument of fortune," which was true either in overcoming the dangers of the road or the inhibiting regulations of the burghers.

In the sixteenth and seventeenth centuries, the commercial movement gained pace because it was favored by the intellectual developments of the Renaissance and the Age of Reason. Philosophies of individualism and secularism, the great wars, and the influx of precious metals added further to its growth. The general outcome was the rise of the state as the basic political unit which subjected municipalities to its superior power. This freed manufacturing and commerce from the guardianship of powerful municipal families and city administrations with the result that competition ran riot. This created many fortunes and forced numerous individuals into bankruptcy.

Again the capitalist turned to a more secure life. The role required a new adventurer for the new times. The old capitalist could rest on his success and turn to careers in state administration. The new capitalist was a gambler and mercantilist in a national economy based on speculation of future profits and imperial investments in transoceanic colonies. Such was the situation when in the late eighteenth century and during the nineteenth century scientific progress and optimism gave rise to the industrial revolution, fostered by the machine and new sources of energy (coal and steam). The international merchant became a part of the landed gentry and the new capitalist, the captain of industry in mining, manufacturing, and investment, came to the fore. It is at this point that Pirenne's description ends.

If one were to continue the description on the basis of the theme of a new capitalist in a new epoch, one could first suggest that the excesses of the nineteenth century capitalist and the imperial national economies of the great powers led to the occurrences of several regulations and modifications. Unionization and humanistic reforms as reactions to child labor, poor wages, unsafe working conditions, etc. clearly limited the exploitive aspects of nineteenth century capitalism. Likewise, international conflicts of economic character, such as wars over imperial holdings or wars of separatism and liberation by the colonized resulted in the gradual demise of the great imperial powers and the establishment of restrictions on international trade. As in earlier times, the capitalist who had amassed a great fortune in portable money retreated to a life of careful investment and his children and grandchildren found occupations of an administrative or diplomatic nature or in philanthropic foundations, or national politics, there to protect the way of life that secured their class.

Where are the new capitalists to be found? Where are those who are marginal to society—exempt from traditional modes and action and restrictions of activity and attitude? Where are the adventurous, the bold, the enterprising of clear intelligence and innovative spirit? What is in demand that only they can produce? What will be their commercial mode? Earlier they were found in the migrant and the declassed. Can Pirenne give us a clue?

> Every class of capitalist is at the beginning animated by a clearly progressive and innovating spirit but becomes conservative as its activities become regulated. To conceive one's self of this truth it is sufficient to recall that the merchants of the eleventh and twelfth centuries are the ancestors of the bourgeoisie and the creators of the first urban institutions; that the businessmen of the Renaissance struggled as energetically as the humanists against social traditions of the Middle Ages; and finally, that those of the nineteenth century have been the most ardent upholders of liberalism.[14]

Also,

> The descendants of the new rich wish to preserve the situation which they have acquired, provided public authority will guarantee it to them, even at the price of

[14] *Ibid.*, pp. 106–107.

troublesome surveillance; they do not hesitate to place their influence at its service, and wait for the moment when, pushed aside by new men, they shall demand of the state that it recognize officially the rank to which they have raised their families . . . and shall consider it beneath them to carry on commerce which in the beginning made their fortunes.[15]

Is Pirenne's analysis correct, and if so, does it provide for prediction? If the answer is yes, one could suggest that the new entrepreneur might be found in the ranks of groups marginal to society, or more specifically, marginal to American life—blacks, Chicanos, Indians, Mafiosa, hippies, etc. Or in other societies, the black marketeers on the streets of Moscow or Da Nang. Or, if that is too far-fetched, an intelligent young man in the back room of a corporation research and development laboratory playing games with a computer. If enterprise is sound in intelligence and has a free rein whether in new products or production techniques, one doubts if it could be found in the executive offices of the modern corporation or a federal bureau.

At any rate, Pirenne's provocative work suggests distinctions between the entrepreneur and the established wealthy. It provides definitions for the concepts we initially linked to the capitalist mode. We can define the entrepreneur as one who embodies the essential requirements of the capitalist man. He starts with nothing and acquires something by virtue of intelligence, marginality, innovation, and risk taking.

To attempt to characterize the capitalist economic system of our time one should take cognizance of some social transformations brought about by previous economic growth which have become endemic and also universal to the western world. The following list embodies basically the ideas of Raymond Aron[16] to which the author has added some probable consequences of these transformations.

---

[15] *Ibid.,* p. 107.

[16] Raymond Aron, *Progress and Disillusion* (New York: New American Library, Mentor, 1968), pp. 237–238.

1. A reduction of the agricultural labor force by a rapid and continuous migration to urban areas. (Result: high urban population density, mechanized farming, unionization of farm workers, and the presence of large corporate farms.)
2. A reduction of the proportion of income spent by individuals for food. (Result: more income freed for leisure activities, nonnecessity items and other products.)
3. An increasing of urbanization of western man. (Result: waste disposal, crime, and transportation problems, and increased interethnic contacts.)
4. Prolongation of the educational process. (Result: longer time before entering the labor market, before marriage, and before the achievement of adult status, leading to prolonged adolescence and a young leisure class.)
5. Shorter working days and careers. (Result: leisure time or multiple careers.)
6. Rapid development of new kinds of industries such as mass media, electronics, computerization, and cybernetics. (Result: further social transformations that only can be imagined.)
7. A diffusion of the means of transportation and communication. (Result: critical pressure on public services as regard common carriers, postal service, and rapid transit.)
8. An increased spending for research and development. (Result: technological innovation which brings us back to number 1 on the list.)

A more general consequence of the social transformations which result from the capitalist mode is that the entrepreneurial function, the work ethic, the motive of acquisition, and the rationalization of production and distribution are themselves in a position of being reevaluated and transformed. Such has been the case since the end of World War II, at which time the above transformations became evident. A very lucid commentary on the economic system in transformation in modern society was made by Joseph Schumpeter in 1947, and it is still quite contemporary in content and attitude.

Most civilizations have disappeared before they had the time to fill the full measure of their promise. Hence I am not going to argue on the strength of that performance, that the capitalist intermezzo is likely to be prolonged. In fact, I am going to draw the exactly opposite inference.[17]

Schumpeter is by no means a foe of capitalism, but on the basis of certain considerations he predicts its demise; or, at least, the demise of the capitalist man of the nineteenth century with whom we are all familiar. The end of this economic mode is predicated on the following conditions elaborated upon by Schumpeter:

1. The obsolescence of the entrepreneurial function.
2. The mechanization of progress.
3. The loss of the capitalist's protective strata.
4. Dysfunction of the large corporate institution.
5. The intellectual climate of criticism produced by capitalism.

To begin with, Schumpeter argues that an eventual near-satiation of economic wants could make the entrepreneurial function obsolete. He realizes, of course, that wants expand and that satisfaction is a "flying goal." However, he notes that the artificial expansion of consumer demands by advertizing may indicate that the automatic supply-demand process might be slowing down. Therefore, there is the logical possibility that capitalism as an evolutionary process could atrophy. There would be nothing left for the entrepreneur to do. "Profits and the rate of interest would converge to zero." This extreme condition would not have to be met, however, by the occurrence of the loss of role for the entrepreneur. A near-satiated consumer situation would impose severe limitations on production and profits. As this begins to occur the entrepreneur is replaced by the administrator. Management of the corporations then becomes a matter of "current administration" and the personnel of the corporation come to acquire more and

---

[17] Joseph Schumpeter, "On Capitalism," in *Images of Man,* ed. C. Wright Mills (New York: George Braziller, 1960), p. 371. The essay, "On Capitalism," was taken from Joseph Schumpeter, *Capitalism, Socialism, and Democracy,* 3rd ed. (New York: Harper and Brothers, 1947).

more the characteristics of bureaucrats. Consequently, a socialism of a "very sober type would come into being." As a maintenance economy emerges, other kinds of pursuits would replace that of economic enterprise in attracting the intelligent and adventurous of society.

Another consequence of near-satiated consumers in a technological age is what Schumpeter refers to as the "mechanization of progress." We have already noted how capitalism relies heavily on the scientific rationalization of production and the creation of new products. The fruits of science are readily utilized in the economic sphere as the entrepreneur seeks to innovate, reform, and revolutionize the pattern of production by exploiting invention in order to "act with confidence beyond the range of familiar beacons." But Schumpeter notes that innovation itself is fast becoming reduced to a patterned routine called research and development. Technological progress and advancement is, in this complex age, becoming the concern of trained specialists who produce what is wanted and make it work in predictable ways. The romance and adventure of an earlier time are going by the board. Economic progress is no longer to be associated with particular men but will become depersonalized and automatic. Committees, boards, task forces, and bureaus are replacing individual decisions and actions, and the new personnel of the industrial bourgeoisie are being reduced to paid administrators. Captains of industry become salaried executives who move from corporation to corporation as hired specialists.

Another of Schumpeter's characterizations consistent with the facts of history is that over time the bourgeoisie has destroyed the protective strata which insured their survival by acting as buffers for the unique social position of the industrial middle class. He notes how the evolution of capitalism quite effectively destroyed the social arrangements of the feudal society. First, the class of artisans and craftsmen were destroyed by automation and competition for cheaply made goods. Second, the classes of lords and peasants were destroyed by bourgeois revolutions aimed at removing all inhibitions to free enterprise. And third, the class of farmers was reduced by the development of large corporate farms aimed at lowering the prices of agricultural commodities. This also resulted in the migration of people to industrial urban areas to form the labor market.

Such changes in society did mean the "breaking of fetters" and removed obstacles to capitalist development. However, as Schumpeter notes, although the fetters hampered the capitalist, they also sheltered his existence. The monarchy managed the state in return for revenues so the bourgeoisie did not have to bother itself with governing. With the demise of monarchies, the bourgeoisie found itself in that position without the necessary talents, time, or charisma to do the job. As Schumpeter puts it, "The stock exchange is a poor substitute for the holy grail." Likewise, the craft guild becomes a workman's union which develops power to equal that of the bourgeoisie.

This condition introduces another which Schumpeter refers to as the "dysfunction of the institutional framework of the capitalist society," or "capitalism undermines its own." Schumpeter is referring here to the deleterious effects of monopolization and the increased largeness in scale of the organizations of enterprise. He notes how large monopolies annihilate the small producers and traders to the point of destroying the entrepreneur. He states, "monopolization plays the role of arteriosclerosis." Its consequences are increasingly unsatisfactory economic performance and economic performance of a political nature.

> The political structure of a nation is profoundly affected by the elimination of a host of small and medium sized firms, the owner-managers of which, together with their dependents, henchmen and connections, count quantitatively at the polls and have a hold on what we may term the foreman class that no management of a large unit can have.[18]

Likewise, with the increasing growth of these large units and the absentee ownership of them by anonymous stockholders, the institutions of private property, free enterprise, and free contracting are also threatened.

Beyond this, in its evolutionary process capitalism has created

---

[18] *Ibid.,* p. 380.

an atmosphere in the west which is yet another problem. Capitalism, since its ascendance as an economic mode, has reinforced critical modes of thought which have destroyed the moral authority of traditional institutions and in the end will turn against capitalism (or it may have already done so). This, coupled with the general incompetence of the bourgeoisie to govern the state, leaves them politically defenseless.

Schumpeter notes how capitalist rationality does not erase the sub- or superrational impulses of the human animal; rather, "it makes them get out of hand by removing the restraints of sacred or semisacred tradition." This leaves a civilization that lacks the means and the will to discipline and guide impulses which lead to nonreasoning revolt.

> Secular improvements that are taken for granted and coupled with individual insecurity that is acutely resented is of course the best recipe for social unrest.[19]

And finally, in the social atmosphere of critical reaction is the central figure of the intellectual—spawned and patronized by the capitalist—who now turns his attention to the capitalist's world.

Schumpeter defines intellectuals as those whose "interest it is to organize resentment." And, capitalism has inevitably created, educated, and subsidized this vested interest in social unrest. He notes how the intellectual operates as a free thinker and critical analyst because he has no direct responsibility for practical affairs. "Capitalism set him loose and provided him with a printing press." The intellectual once worked for the church, then for the entrepreneur, and now he works for public opinion. Interestingly enough, the freedom of thought of which the capitalist now disapproves cannot be crushed without crushing the freedom that the capitalist approves and requires for his existence.

One may well want to express certain criticisms of the analyses of Pirenne and Schumpeter. Initially, one cannot gloss over uncritically the hypothesis of Pirenne concerning the replacement of one social type by another. For one thing, the description of the process does not consider enough conditions to allow for predic-

---

[19] *Ibid.*, p. 384.

tion of the nature of continued development. Likewise, one cannot uncritically accept Schumpeter's analysis wholly in light of the biases he implies, such as his characterization of intellectuals (he may be correct, however).

After considering certain criticisms, one must recognize the contributions provided which aid our understanding of this particular system enterprise. It is in the characterizations of Pirenne and Schumpeter that we find contextual definitions for the concepts and assumptions that are traditionally associated with analyses of capitalism in economic theory which can now be summarized in a description of capitalism as an abstract process in interface with religion, politics, science and western man's demographic transitions. Concomitant with the transitions in the economic life of western man through history have been transitions of beliefs, philosophies, governments, knowledge banks, and the size and distribution of populations. Some theorists have seen changes in these other sectors as the causes of the new economic modes, others have portrayed the economic mode (Marx in particular) as the efficient cause of change in all other sectors. Neither of these approaches of one-sided causality provides a satisfactory explanation. When and if a satisfactory explanation becomes a reality, it will probably be one which reveals a relation of interdependence between all of these factors operating in a fluid system.

From the review of the works of Schumpeter and Pirenne one can appreciate the complexity of the problem. However, one can also see a description of the capitalist process emerging. It can be seen that the concept and reality of private property gives rise to an ethic of acquisitiveness which, given the development of a money standard, gives rise to the necessity for accounting and the ethic of profit in an uninhibited market where supply and demand dictate prices. It can be seen also that in order to remove the inhibitions of tradition a critical utilitarianism develops. But the break with tradition and the rise of more pragmatic and democratic philosophies mean that the fruits of capitalist industry must have wider distribution (distributive justice) as the worker gains an awareness of the value of his labor. Likewise, it has been seen that the critical philosophies unleash intellectual activity from the bonds of dogma, giving rise to scientific and technological development which can be exploited by the industrialist to increase productivity or to create new goods, markets, and raw materials. Concomitant with these changes are the increase in populations and the steady migration of these populations to urban centers of activity where transformations constantly make new demands upon economic and political systems.

In a previous chapter, we also saw how the Protestant Reformation with its dimensions of pietism and puritanism (personal salvation by working in this world) gave rise to a workmanship ethic that so neatly met the developing needs of capitalist enterprise for a free and ample labor supply. But it is also apparent that at the present stage, the need to work is met by a fairly widespread reality of increased leisure time provided by a highly efficient technology. It is also becoming apparent that in our time when the needs for private commodities could near the satiation point the communal needs for public services are far from being met. Can the entrepreneur capitalize on this new market? Can a market be created for clean air, public transportation, livable cities, potable water, and spiritual security?

Chapter 15 The Enterprise of Law and Politics: The Distribution of Power

Preacher took a swig at the bottle and went on, "I'm no simple peasant, brother; I don't come from the servile class; I'm a deacon's son, and when I was free I lived in Kursk and used to go around in a frock coat; but now I've brought myself to such a point that I can sleep naked on the ground and eat grass. And God give everyone such a life. I don't want anything, I'm not afraid of anyone, and the way I see it, there's no man richer or freer than I am."[1]

This chapter deals with the system of governmental and legal activity. As with the other systems already discussed, there is in

[1] Anton Chekhov, "In Exile," 1892, in *Anton Chekhov, Selected Stories,* ed. and trans. Ann Dunnigan (New York: New American Library, 1960), p. 124.

this system an ethos, technical requirements, actors, goals, general system commodities, and a product.

The basic technical requirement is that of establishing a political system which orders the daily relationships and activities of a complex multitude of people who occupy a specific geographic area. Such agglomerates range from tribes, to cities, to states, to nations, to international alliances.

Classifications of the actors involved may be as simple as a distinction between rulers and ruled, elites and non-elites, or it can be as complex a classification as the political scientist or theorist has time and energy to construct, for example, elites, politicians, legislators, executives, voters, publics, mobs, masses, etc.

The individual and shared goals of the political enterprise are diverse. However, power and security characterize all political systems because they embody nearly all other goals of political man as he seeks to insure his survival and promote his self-interest. Therefore, the commodities of the political system are those which satisfy the need for power and security. Security, which may also be called freedom from fear, is sometimes exchanged for power. For example, the voter often says to the politician, "Give me some assurance that my interests will be shown concern and I will give you my vote."

The product of the political enterprise is the establishment and maintenance of some form of social-economic order. Such an order (of which there are numerous historical types) results from the creation of a legal structure which establishes a distribution of power in codified form. The established order also legitimates or creates an acceptance of the legal structure. A necessary requisite for this legal structure is that it also must include a codification of how wealth and property may be distributed. Consensus about the legitimacy of this distribution may be arrived at by force, or by an agreement among the people that such an arrangement is inclusive of their interests.

Consensus about the nature of the structure will be arrived at if enough members of the group believe that the structure is beneficial to them. This, of course, assumes that they have enough sophistication to make such a judgment. Another way to establish legitimacy short of naked force and the use of terror is for members of the collective to be convinced that by the use of cultural symbols or propaganda the existing order is beneficial to them or will eventually serve their interests. When the masses are not sophisticated, they are generally subservient to a ruling class.

In modern industrial societies of the west there exists a high level of sophistication and literacy. Instead of masses and collectives we generally find publics and constituents. When major social and economic interests are involved in the creation of public policy a shared definition of legitimacy will result. Such an order is generally referred to as pluralist democracy. Pluralist democracy is still an ideal type, but enough of the dimensions of such a type exist to allow political sociologists and political scientists to make judgments about its efficacy.

Therefore, in drawing the boundaries of the modern political system the author will confine his description of the ethos of the political system to the dimensions of pluralist democracy. These dimensions may or may not be in agreement with the descriptions of many contemporary theorists and commentators. However, it is the author's judgment that the following dimensions characterize the system in question, although they are often violated.

1. Representation and the circulation of responsible elites.
2. Individual civic responsibility.
3. Civil participation.
4. Legal universalism and rationalism.

REPRESENTATION AND THE CIRCULATION OF RESPONSIBLE ELITES   At the outset, the reader ought to be reminded that there are differences between individuals which create an unequal distribution of political activity and influence. This, of course, means a distinction between rulers and ruled, representatives and represented, and elites and publics.

The most cogent argument about these differences is given by Robert Dahl in *Modern Political Analysis*.[2] He makes certain assumptions as follows:

[2] Robert A. Dahl, *Modern Political Analysis* (Englewood Cliffs, N. J.: Prentice-Hall, 1963), p. 17. Copyright © 1964. By permission of the publisher, Prentice-Hall, Inc.

1. People exhibit differences in mental and biological endowments and in life experiences.
2. These differences lead to differences in the economic and hence political resources and the motivations of individuals.
3. This in turn leads to differences in political skills and the extent to which resources at hand are used for the acquisition of political influence and the use of this influence.
4. This, then, results in differences in political influence or power.
5. This differential distribution of influence leads to differences in endowments and experiences of one's progeny—and the cycle continues.

For example, if a society was marked by two groups, the highly endowed and the non-endowed, the resulting governmental structure would be a monarchy or tyranny; ruling elites and masses. It is generally believed that the most important characteristic of a pluralist democracy is the presence of universal education. Modern societies are, therefore, made up largely of people who are highly endowed and those with average-to-high endowment. Instead of masses there are debating publics who have an understanding, concern, and knowledge of when and how their interests are represented. The result is constituencies whose interests are defined in the legislature by elected representatives, rather than masses held in control by tyrannical elites.

A pluralist democracy is not designed to give legislative representation to every individual's whims and prerogatives. In theory, however, it ideally gives representation to all major autonomous regional or interest groups. This ideal is realized with varying amounts of success in reality.

The realization by many of today's youths that the legislative representative is more available to the wealthy lobbyist than he is to the others who are less well organized and who have less financial backing has become a source of renewed vigor in public debate and reaction. When policies are made without a real public consensus, the result is often political alienation and distrust. Some commentators have suggested that in a modern technological society there is no longer a debating public because people have become educated with such specialization that the political acumen or interest is not sufficient for civic participation. Schematically these relationships could be shown as follows:

Endowments and Experiences

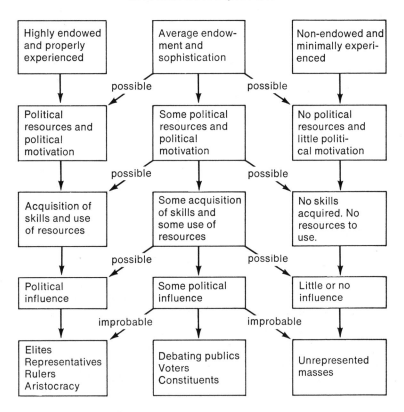

At this point a summarization of the thoughts of Karl Mannheim concerning the "fundamental democratization" of western societies might give perspective to this problem.[3] Mannheim saw two processes at work in western society: fundamental democracy

[3] Karl Mannheim, "Rational and Irrational Elements in Contemporary Society," in *Man in Contemporary Society,* ed. William R. Taber (New York: Columbia University Press, 1962), pp. 330–356.

and interdependence. Mannheim believed that the consequences of these revolutionary processes have not been fully appreciated because until recently we have labored under the false belief that the national character is permanent and that there is a gradual process of reason in history. The problem of some modern democracies, as Mannheim saw it, was that reason and moral purpose are not distributed evenly throughout a society. "Reason progresses only as long as social structure fulfills certain conditions of harmonious growth"—that is, moral and educational development should keep pace with technological development to preserve harmony.

He suggests that a society too quickly democratized makes impotent the groups which previously ruled society and in whom were entrusted the reins of reason and moral understanding. In so doing, the power of the irrational is unleashed. No doubt Mannheim was reacting to the Third Reich in Germany, the Bolshevik Revolution, and the Stalinists in Russia. One of Mannheim's main theses was:

> The contemporary social order must collapse if rational social control and the individual's mastery over his own impulses do not keep step with technological development.[4]

The industrial and technological age in the west has created at least two severe kinds of disproportion according to Mannheim. First, the development of scientific knowledge has proceeded to a point where it surpasses the moral powers of man and his insight into social forces. We have great destructive powers in hand without the moral insight to make decisions about their use. Second, there is a disproportionate distribution of rational and moral capacities in human society. Those who have such capacities may not be in a position to utilize them.

Another thesis of Mannheim's was:

> The unfolding of reason, the ordering of impulse and the form taken by morality are, by no means, an

---

[4] *Ibid.,* p. 333.

accident.... They depend on the problems set by the existing order of society.[5]

In other words, the existing order of society favors certain groups and condemns others to passivity. Society does so by assigning certain roles to one group which require decision-making ability (reason and moral understanding) while the rest are left to "adjust themselves to their position only by renouncing all insight and initiative."

In modern society the formerly passive classes have suddenly been stirred into action in the political arena. Mannheim calls this fundamental democratization. The implication is that the activity of the masses who most probably do not have the powers of reason and moral understanding for making decisions in this age have now come to center stage in political processes. This is not to say, however, that such groups could not increase their capacities. There are historical cases where power by the masses preceded understanding with rather disastrous effects, especially in those cases where the masses turned against the leaders who had first stirred them to action.

At any rate, Western history, since the Enlightenment at least, has been characterized by a growing number of social groups seeking to share in social-political control. And, initially at least, they come from "intellectually backward" groups and constitute a threat to the elites who traditionally "sought to keep the masses at a low intellectual level."[6] In this way "Irrationalism forces its way into the arena of public life ... even dominating that arena."[7]

Mannheim also indicated that democracy can and has led to rational behavior insofar as political power was initially granted only to the propertied and educated classes and then only gradually to the proletariat. One might suggest that this has been the case in Great Britain and in the United States to a great extent. When the shift of power has been more dramatic, it has resulted in negative consequences. "Any dominant group which has been naive enough to believe that it made use of these

[5] *Ibid.*
[6] *Ibid.*, p. 334.
[7] *Ibid.*

energies will soon find itself being pushed instead of doing the pushing."[8] Mannheim was convinced that any society which suffered from uneven distribution of rational insight would experience instability. The suggestion is, therefore, that a prerequisite of democracy is universal education. "Either one desires democracy and attempts to bring everyone into similar levels of understanding or one reverses the democratization process."[9]

He notes that most post-revolutionary elites do just that— reverse the process of democratization. In so doing, the intellectual and executive activities "become bureaucratized to the last degree as power is concentrated in a centralized few."[10] Mannheim goes on to list the ways in which social power (political and economic as well) is monopolized in reversing the democratization process.

1. The possession of social knowledge and the power to make policy decisions are centralized within a relatively small coterie of political figures, industrial leaders, administrators, and legal authorities.
2. A bureaucratic class may come into existence which is separate and distinct from other classes in the society.
3. There could then also be a centralization of the instrumentalities of military power of the society.

Furthermore, notes Mannheim, "The political as well as the economic bureaucracy will be able to cope with the complicated machinery of society as long as it can be sure to a certain degree of the acquiescence of small personal groups collecting in the pursuit of common interests."[11] Which is to say, the centralized elite must still legitimate the order and its own existence.

Coincidental to the process of fundamental democratization there has occurred what Mannheim calls the process of increasing interdependence—what one might call the rise of the Swiss watch society. As industrial man becomes highly specialized in his

[8] *Ibid.*, p. 335.
[9] *Ibid.*, p. 336.
[10] *Ibid.*
[11] *Ibid.*, p. 337.

occupational role, the division of labor becomes highly complex which results in a high degree of interdependence of each role on the other. If particular roles are not played, or played badly, the mechanism will not function properly. Says Mannheim, "Modern society can absorb irrational and emotional shocks less easily than earlier social orders,"[12] for there is less margin for slippage. When situations favor certain forms of egoism and recklessness the results are nondemocratic.

One danger of the interdependent society is that great sophistication is necessary to make decisions about far-reaching policy, but, says Mannheim, "nobody plans the planners." In this light one remembers the anecdote about the newly chosen economic adviser to an American president who had expressed certain misgivings to his friend about his ability to handle this responsibility. His friend replied, "Don't worry—remember, the President doesn't know what you're talking about either."

Elite Circulation   A closely related aspect of representation in a pluralist system is a circulating elite. The notion is that governmental figures should be periodically changed in an orderly fashion. Such a concept is codified in the American constitution, in which the length of terms of office is established. However, such a code deals mainly with visible functionaries of government which may not be the political-economic elite at all. A commentary on the pervasive nature of elites by C. Wright Mills will be discussed a bit later.

What is the western ideal of elites in the age of democratization? The revolutionary nature of this ideal is that they are elites of ability and responsibility, rather than elites of inherited charisma or elites by virtue of primogeniture, or blood line. José Ortega y Gasset has made an interesting commentary on this ideal. He paints a rather pessimistic picture concerning the future of noble endeavor.

> . . . there is no doubt that the most radical division that
> is possible to make of humanity is that which splits it

---

[12] *Ibid.*

into two classes of creatures: those who make great demands on themselves, piling up difficulties and duties; and those who demand nothing special of themselves, but for whom to live is to be every moment what they already are, without imposing upon themselves any effort towards perfection; mere buoys that float on the waves.[13]

Having thus established for us his classification of mankind into masses and select minorities, he also points out that these are not necessarily identical with upper and lower socioeconomic classes. The two types are found in both classes.

The continuing notion in Ortega y Gasset is that modern catastrophies can be attributed to the ascendance of the masses and the impotence of the select minority. He says, "Heretofore the mass asserted no right to intervene in the special activities of the qualified minority. They realized that if they wished to intervene they would necessarily have to acquire those special qualities and cease being mere mass. They recognized their place in a healthy dynamic system."[14]

One could raise the question whether earlier orders were really healthy and dynamic, but his assessment of the modern phenomena is relatively accurate as Ortega y Gasset goes on to describe how the mass has in certain systems moved into the foreground of social life, occupying social positions, utilizing social instruments, and enjoying the pleasures heretofore enjoyed only by the select few. His fear is that the nouveau classes do not have the civility to do this without some dire consequences for modern civilization. He notes:

The old democracy was tempered by a generous dose of liberalism and enthusiasm for law. By serving these principles the individual bound himself to maintain a severe discipline over himself. Under the shelter of

[13] José Ortega y Gasset, "The Revolt of the Masses," in *Man in Contemporary Society*, ed. William R. Taber (New York: Columbia University Press, 1962), p. 487.
[14] *Ibid.*, p. 488.

liberal principles and the rule of law, minorities could live and act.[15]

But this has been replaced with what Ortega y Gasset refers to as a "hyper-democracy" in which the mass acts directly and outside the law in such a way as to impose its interests by physical pressure.

> The mass believes that it has the right to impose and to give force of law to notions born in a cafe. . . . The characteristic of the hour is that the commonplace mind, moving itself to be commonplace, has the assurance to proclaim the rights of the commonplace and to impose it whenever they will . . . to be different is to be indecent.[16]

INDIVIDUAL CIVIC RESPONSIBILITY   Another dimension of the pluralist ethos is that of civic responsibility. As an ideal it connotes a demand that society provide institutions for a sophisticated electorate and that each constituent is duty bound to be advised about the state of the nation. Max Weber has discussed this issue within the framework of three conceptual distinctions: (1) the ethic of ultimate ends, (2) the ethic of responsibility, and (3) the calling of politics.

Weber's sociological insights make him a realist and this realism fosters a moral philosophy of political behavior that is at once idealistic and pragmatic. In Weber's analysis, the citizen's action is promoted by an ethic of ultimate ends while the political decision-maker is motivated by the ethic of responsibility.[17] Weber comments:

> Politics is a strong and slow boring of hardboards. It takes both passion and perspective . . . and even those

---

[15] *Ibid.,* p. 489.

[16] *Ibid.*

[17] These particular aspects of Weber's thought can be found in *From Max Weber: Essays in Sociology,* eds. H. H. Gerth, and C. W. Mills (New York: Oxford University Press, 1946), pp. 77–128. See also, Raymond Aron, *German Sociology* (New York: The Free Press, 1964), pp. 82–92; and Julien Freund, *The Sociology of Max Weber* (New York: Random, Vintage, 1969), pp. 28–32.

who are neither leaders nor heroes must arm themselves with that steadfastness of heart which can
brave even the crumbling of hopes ... only he has the
calling for politics who is sure that he shall not
crumble when the world from his point of view is too
stupid or too base for what he wants to offer.[18]

By politics Weber means the "leadership and the influencing
of leadership" in the modern state. And he defines the modern
political association or state "in terms of specific means peculiar
to it"—the use of physical force. The state to Weber is a community of actors who successfully lay claim to a monopoly of the
legitimate use of physical force within a particular geographic
area. The right to use force is ascribed to particular social institutions or to individuals by permission of the state adherent to its
codes. Therefore, politics means to Weber "the striving to share
power or striving to influence the distribution of power" among
states or within states. He defines power as that which enables a
group or individual to make his will manifested in the social
collective. The sociological questions which arise are also
questions of morality. For the state to exist, those who are
dominated must obey those in authority. When and why do men
obey? Upon what inner justifications and upon what external
means does the domination rest?

Weber offers three kinds of inner justifications or basic
legitimizations of domination.

The first he calls the authority of the "eternal yesterday"
which is essentially traditional authority. These are "mores
sanctified by time."

The second is the authority of the "gift of grace" or charismatic authority; that is, authority maintained by virtue of the
personal appeal of the leader in question.

The third is authority which is maintained by virtue of a belief
among the constituents in the validity of the legal statutes of
the state wherein logic and rationality are brought to bear.

There are four external means of maintaining domination or
power:

[18] Gerth, and Mills, p. 128. (See footnote 17.)

1. Power is held by maintaining control of the distribution of material rewards in a community.
2. Power is held by maintaining a policy which is in line with the traditional and present prerogatives of the society's members.
3. Power is held by maintaining a monopoly over the use of force and the instruments of force.
4. Power is held by maintaining a monopoly of knowledge. Competence makes one indispensable.

If one seeks to be politically active there are two general paths of action depending on the ethic one subscribes to: ultimate ends or responsibility. Both are found in the traditional religion of the West, where there is a precedent for both moral principles. The ethic of ultimate ends is: "The Christian acts rightly and leaves the results with the Lord"; or, he "follows the maxim of responsibility, in which case he has to give an account of the foreseeable results of his action." The ethic of ultimate ends is referred to by Raymond Aron as the "ethic of inspiration," and as the "ethic of conviction" by Julien Freund. It is an action framework that includes more than the simple dictum that the "ends justify the means." One who acts according to this ethic follows the conviction that an act is necessary, but he does not have real understanding of the consequences. Therefore, it is of lesser moral value than the action framework of responsibility.

Weber believed that political philosophies ought to be predicated on the assumption that "we try our best to change the world in the direction we desire . . . to avoid bringing about in the last resort a situation contrary to that at which we aimed."[19] That good can really come from good, or will always result from good was considered a logical non sequitur by Weber. He noted the paradox that the prophet of love is condemned to simply prophecy or to the contradictory action of advocating a final recourse to violence in order to establish the reign of love. A real leader feels "responsible for what he allows to be done as well as for what he does himself. He has the courage of truth and not merely a sense of opportunity." Genuine politics does not re-

[19] Aron, p. 84. (See footnote 17.)

pudiate moral forces. Necessarily, political actions will affect large numbers of people; therefore, says Weber, they must be rejected as soon as they threaten the dignity of the human being. The proponent of the ethic of responsibility bears in mind what is possible and looks for the most appropriate means for achieving the desired end, while keeping in mind his responsibility to others. On the other hand, those who act on the basis of an unconditional morality of all or nothing (who assume without proof that the consequences will be good because they are pure of heart) will, when faced with resolute opposition, allegate their powerlessness to human stupidity and a base world and hence have a personal justification for advocating violence. Those who act on the basis of responsibility are those who have the understanding to know that the consequences do not cease at the command of him who initiates the action.

CIVIL PARTICIPATION   The third dimension of the ethos of western political systems is that of civil rights. This deals with the delicate balance between general society-wide solidarity and freedom for the individual; that is, how much constraint is necessary for maintaining order and how much freedom is necessary for maintaining creative individual action? At what point does lack of order inhibit the individual as much as too much order would? These questions will be debated for decades to come. However, there are some practical questions which can be discussed concerning the nature of justice. Justice has become legalized in western cultures in constitutions, as in the Bill of Rights.

The conflict between the minority of one and the majority of the propertied represents a major ongoing contradiction in the political systems of the West. This problem comes to the fore when the debate arises over who shall be involved in making the decisions which will affect the whole social system. Do we simply assume that the propertied elites know what they are doing and give them the major share in this activity? A most intriguing modern commentary on this situation is in C. Wright Mills's *The Power Elite.*

The picture drawn by Mills is essentially that the major decision-making prerogative resides in a handful of men in industry, the military, and government. One infers from Mills that civil rights may be threatened by such a process of increased centralization of society's administration. As he notes in the introductory paragraph:

> The powers of ordinary men are circumscribed by the everyday worlds in which they live, yet even in their rounds of job, family, and neighborhood they often seem driven by forces they can neither understand nor govern.[20]

He goes on to note how the traditional institutions which acted as buffers of power between the elites and ordinary men have lost their potency.

> Families and churches and schools adapt to modern life; governments and armies and corporations shape it; and as they do so, they turn these lesser institutions into means for their ends. . . . The symbols of all these lesser institutions are used to legitimate the power and decisions of the big three.[21]

In a manner somewhat reminiscent of Mannheim's conceptualization of the reversal of fundamental democratization, Mills notes how "within each of the big three, the typical institutional unit has become enlarged, has become administrative, and, in the power of its decision has become centralized."[22]

Mills's conceptualization of the power elite rests upon the observation of particular trends that he feels characterize our age.[23] Such trends are: (1) ascendance of the military in a (2) privately incorporated economy, along with (3) the coincidence of similar interests shared by economic, military, and political sectors of our society. Likewise, he notes that there are (4) essential "social similarities and psychological affinities" among the men who are in these "command posts" of these sectors of modern

[20] C. Wright Mills, *The Power Elite* (New York: Oxford University Press, Galaxy, 1959), p. 3.
[21] *Ibid.*, p. 6.
[22] *Ibid.*, p. 7.
[23] *Ibid.*, p. 296.

society. He notes that there is "interchangeability" of the top positions of the big three and an "increased traffic between these orders in the careers of men of power." Such an observation was made later by Domhoff, who adds substantiation to many of Mills's hypotheses, in his study, *Who Rules America?*[24] The result of this is (5) a group of men who "by training and bent are professional organizers of considerable force and who are unrestrained by democratic party training."[25]

Further consequences of this are that (6) the professional party politician is active only in the middle ranges of power concerning matters of secondary importance. There also exists what Mills calls (7) the "semi-organized stalemate of interests of sovereign localities into which the legislative function has fallen."[26] Along with this is (8) the demise of competent and skilled civil service with its politically neutral repertory of brainpower, and (9) the increased amount of official secrecy which veils the great decisions that are made—made without benefit of public or congressional debate which is a necessary aspect of pluralist democracy. The only place where pluralism prevails is in the middle ranges of social activity. Mills is convinced that the elites are not representative men; that there is not one elite of noble endeavor, moral virtue, or meritorious activity. They are selected and formed by the "means of power, the sources of wealth and the mechanisms of celebrity." Likewise, Mills does not see them as being held in check by a plurality of interest groups or by debating publics. "Unqualified in human history, they have succeeded within the American system of organized irresponsibility."[27]

William Kornhauser's commentary on modern political behavior written in 1959 adds another dimension to the Mills critique.[28] Kornhauser describes a trend which appears to char-

---

[24] William G. Domhoff, *Who Rules America?* (Englewood, N. J.: Prentice-Hall, 1967).

[25] Mills, *op. cit.*, p. 296.

[26] *Ibid.*

[27] *Ibid.*, p. 361.

[28] William Kornhauser, "The Structure of Mass Society," in *Man and Contemporary Society*, ed. William R. Taber (New York: Columbia University Press, 1962), pp. 532–555.

acterize western industrial societies; namely, that they may become mass or atomized societies—societies in which members are "interconnected only by virtue of their common ties to national centers of communication and organizations." Such a society is characterized by primary groups which are isolated from the larger society and cannot provide the basis for the involvement of the individual in the larger society. Whatever people feel ought to be undertaken is simply "heaped onto the state." The result is a highly centralized all-inclusive decision-making national administration. Intermediary interest groups which connected the individual to the elites and acted as buffers for both diminish. They, hence, become directly exposed to one another and mass behavior marks the relationship which was heretofore filtered through the intervening groups of a pluralist society. Access to elites in a pluralist society exists by virtue of independence from them and the independence exists by virtue of a multiplicity of associations no one of which is inclusive of its members' lives. The consequent oppositions between groups restrain their relative power and limit the ascendance to total power of any group. However, as the intermediate associations diminish in a mass society there occurs increased centralization in national administration and decreased accessibility to the elites. Mass society can then turn into totalitarianism and civil rights, which become secondary to the prerogatives of the power elite. Maintenance of strong and multiple voluntary associations of interest groups ranging from unions to political parties would insure access to the elites, limit the powers of the elites and force restraint upon the non-elites. The outcome of this would ideally be the maintenance of a pluralist democratic political system.

LEGAL UNIVERSALISM AND RATIONALISM The final dimension of the political system ethos is universalism and rationalism in jurisprudence, or the institutionalization of justice. For definitions and concepts regarding this dimension, we turn to *Max Weber on Law and Economy in Society.*[29]

[29] Max Rheinstein, *Max Weber on Law and Economy in Society* (New York: Simon and Schuster, Clarion, 1967).

Weber demonstrates how western law has grown out of Roman concepts of justice and the rational-formalism of German law. Involved in rational-formalism are two basic concepts: one, universal application of the law no matter what the characteristics of the offender might be, and two, what constitutes evidence in the judgment of guilt or innocence. Along with this is the ideal of the uses of rational and logical processes in the creation of law and in using legal precedents to formulate a case. Implied in Weber's discussion is a typology of judicial action which aids in distinguishing legal rationalism from other legal-judicial systems that have existed.

Legal rationalism itself has two aspects: (1) the formal aspect —general rules in the abstract and a philosophy of justice, and (2) the substantive aspect—characteristic action in the real situations of political-legal life which may sometimes contradict formal requirements and in which winning the case may sometimes be of more importance to the actors involved than are the principles of justice. The following table outlines such distinctions.

Creating Law and Finding Law

	Formal	Substantive
Rational	Significance is ascribed to operative facts dictated by principles of evidence and applied abstractly in deciding the case.	The process follows general principles from the areas of religion or ethical ideology.
Irrational	Judgment of significance concerning factors in the case are beyond the control of reason; i.e., the use of oracles, revelation, or ordeals in deciding the case.	The process does not adhere to general norms or principles. It is arbitrary and particularistic (jumping to conclusions).

In general, the legal structure of the west is marked by the formal rational ideal; however, the contingencies of the actual situation usually dictate the rational substantive. In any case, rationalism marks the ideal of Western legal action, but deviations from this ideal are sometimes found. Righteous reaction, arbitrariness, particularism, improper use of evidence or lack of proper evidence can be and often are grounds for appealing a legal decision. Weber notes that there are other carry-overs from the irrational systems of earlier days. One in particular that we maintain as a tradition in legal activity is the convention of not giving the reasons for a verdict from the bench or from the jury once the case is decided. Weber notes this as a contradiction to rational-formalism and is a convention more suited to decisions by revelation.[30] He also notes how particularism still is a factor in judicial behavior. "The propertyless classes in particular are not served in the way in which the bourgeois are by formal legal equality and calculated adjudication and administration."[31] Since Weber's time, however, great strides have been made, especially in U.S. jurisprudence. The ideal has not been attained, but the ideal exists. It was only in 1963 that the U.S. Supreme Court held that "the mere existence of a serious criminal charge constituted in itself special circumstances requiring the services of counsel at trial." Independent of the ability of the defendent to employ legal counsel, then, one will be provided. It was only in 1932 that this was done for defendants in capital crimes.[32]

INTERFACE WITH OTHER SYSTEMS   The probabilities of negative feedback in system interface are implicit in the drawings of the system boundaries of the political enterprise. In general, the implications force us to question rather than to answer. As yet there are more hypotheses regarding political behavior and action than there are operative facts. However, to know the questions aids in anticipating the future of modern systems. The questions and tentative answers have been stated by the critics and commentators whose ideas were used in the preceding pages. Some of the questions are:

[30] *Ibid.,* p. 351.
[31] *Ibid.,* p. 355.
[32] Delmar Karlen, *The Citizen in Court* (New York: Harcourt Brace Jovanovich, 1965), p. 48.

1. What continuing effect will scientific and technological advances have on the nature of political realities and hence on the distribution of power and the freedom of the individual?
2. What will be the future of religious and ethical ideology in the face of increased rationalism? Must not moral philosophy be a consideration in political action?
3. Can the ideals of pluralist democracy be met in a system marked by a privately incorporated economy, or is such an economy detrimental to the attainment of these ideals? May not a communal economy be just as detrimental?
4. What is the nature of educational processes that would insure the existence of debating publics essential to pluralism and erase the spectre of the destructive masses?
5. Can a sociologist approach the study of politics without taking a value position?
6. "Is democracy possible in an age when decisions are so complex?"[33]
7. "Can the populous be educated enough to make decisions on the basis of understanding the complex interrelationships between sub-systems?"[34]

[33] See John McDermott, "Technocracy: The Opiate of the Intellectuals" in *The New York Review of Books* (July, 1969).
[34] *Ibid.*

Chapter 16 The New Sociology

One of the first things which any scientist learns when he attempts to become involved in practical affairs in order to use his scientific ideas to control natural events is the inevitable gap between theory and practice. Just as we must not expect most physicists to be able to build bridges, however much the building of bridges actually benefits from a knowledge of the scientific principles involved in calculating stresses, so we must not expect most social scientists to be able to solve social problems.[1]

Since the fall of 1968 a plethora of paperback titles has hit the book market bearing front covers festooned with imagery and

[1] Jack Douglas, *The Relevance of Sociology* (New York: Appleton-Century-Crofts, 1970), p. 203.

symbols proclaiming novel approaches to courses in sociology. Many of these have been anthologies containing articles depicting the sixties as a decade of change or revolution. The words radical, revolution, action, are most common. Art layouts range from psychedelic "65" to the fantasy of Peter Max and include many of the symbols from the language of the so-called "turned on youth." It is rare, however, that what is found inside reflects the novelty of the cover.

There have been a few works of single authors which speak to present situations not so much with novel concepts but with novel presentation and application of concepts that have been with the discipline for some time. Thomas Wolfe, Herbert Marcuse, Franz Fanon, Paul Goodman, and Theodore Roszak are authors who catch the interest of young, would-be sociologists. Interestingly, the above are probably not considered bona fide sociologists by themselves or the discipline. They are writers and philosophers who have discovered the radical nature of sociology and its concepts—a radical nature that has been with the discipline on and off since about 1820.

In the latter part of August, 1969 the American Sociological Association convened in San Francisco and its members were confronted with a number of youthful initiates to the discipline who demonstrated varying degrees of frustration and antipathy toward the established Ph.D.s whom they considered were not acting in good faith. The essence of their concern could probably be boiled down to "If you're so smart, why are there wars, inequality, pestilence, ecological crises, ghettos, and unacceptable conditions in our prisons and medical facilities?"

As novel as all the above reactions appear, they may be the essence of the new student, but they are not the essence of the new sociology. The various mobilizations of the sixties have made contributions to the new sociology but they are not part and parcel of it. Likewise, take away all the ballyhoo and the new sociology is really not new either in terms of concerns and concepts or attempts at real world relevance.

What is the new sociology? Or, more honestly, what does this writer take the new sociology to be? In this chapter, which concludes this introduction to sociology, a definition and description will be attempted on the basis of present concerns, novel concepts, and, although the word is meaningless unless followed by a preposition and object, relevance.

Concerns   Since its beginnings and through its various periods— Enlightenment, German Romanticism, Marxian Determinism, Reaction to Marx, American Pragmatism, and the Age of Empiricism —the discipline of sociology has been humanely and rationally concerned with the realities of human society. Apart from the methods of answering questions which are most obvious, there is a less obvious collection of questions that deal with justice and humanism. As in all other bodies of knowledge, the fruits of sociological inquiry have not always been utilized by just and humane men.

The works of western literati have often asked these questions of justice and humanity. From Dickens to the muckrakers to Cleaver, the theme of justice which has been longed for but rarely experienced is most obvious. But it is in the social sciences that answers are sought. In light of the observation that wrong answers have wrought disastrous effects, the concern has been (until very recently) with the *methods* of inquiry and not as much as with the *questions.* The demand on the social sciences in the seventies is going to be with answers and their application; it is a pressing demand. One only hopes that because of the pressing demand, the answers will not be premature. Too much of the end product up to now has resulted from the unanticipated consequences of well-planned action. Solving problems sometimes causes greater ones.

Apart from the all-embracing concern for human justice, the special concerns of the new sociology will deal with research and conceptual work in the areas of inter-ethnic contact, preservation of ethnic diversity, and the ecosystem or global life support system as it relates to the social systems, war and aggression, poverty, population, and the social-psychological salvation of post-industrial man.

Concepts   The concepts of the new sociology will be marked by a more interdisciplinary character than they have been for the last few decades. An increased concern for the concepts from the fields of animal behavior or ethology, linguistics, psychology, physical systems, political analysis, and economics are in evidence at the beginning of the decade of the seventies. Some of these are nineteenth century models; some are truly novel. Hall's "proxemics" and Boulding's iconometrics are some special areas of conceptual novelty that are intriguing to the sociologist. More time will be spent with these later in the chapter.

Relevance (of something to something)   When youthful students of sociology demand relevance, the usual statement carries little meaning. "The relevance of what to what" is a normal professorial reply to what is either an inquisitive or accusatory statement. And the usual reply by students to that is "you are irrelevant to my education." Some critics of higher education (James Coleman and Marshall McLuhan come to mind) have defined the criteria of relevance, and any discipline hoping to make a contribution must pay them some heed.

1. Is the course of study relevant to the extended life realities of the student? Is the student receiving any practical preparation? Does he want any?
2. Are we using the most practical media for conveying and teaching ideas or skills? Can a tape recorder or super-i projector do what we do and do it better? If so, maybe we should be doing something else.
3. Are the courses of study related to some greater social eschatos—progress, justice, survival, etc.
4. Does it make any difference?

Therefore, as sociology moves into the last quarter of the twentieth century, the renewed concerns, the refurbished concepts, and the focus on the relevance of sociology for a changing society of technical man will most probably be demonstrated in research and teaching activity that places renewed emphasis on demographic studies, population growth, and education and socialization.

Renewed Emphasis on Demographic Studies   In a very general way, one could define demography as the study of change in statistical populations, human and nonhuman. It has been a sub-discipline of biology, sociology, and geography for at least two centuries, and presently it is becoming a specialized discipline in its own right. Even as it becomes an autonomous discipline the accumulation of information it provides becomes of great value to sociology, because as a number of population factors are opera-tionalized and made available to research, this will greatly promote highly reliable investigation, which is essential to the continued growth of sociological theory.

A brief list of variables which aid us in understanding the popu-lation base of the social system would include: population density in specific geographic areas or specific ecological space; rates of natural increase of populations; rates of nativity (births); rates of morbidity (deaths); rates of migration (in and out of a population area); growth trends of population and the racial, ethnic, eco-nomic, political, and psychological characteristics of populations and how such characteristics are distributed. Closely related to these concerns is the demographic offspring—epidemiology—or the study of statistical rates of physical and mental illnesses which characterize populations. Equally important, but not yet as reliable, are the uniform crime statistics which characterize populations.

Statistical information has become of great concern among a variety of disciplines, and this concern has resulted in a more interdisciplinary approach to the explanations of the problematic relationships between human populations and their physical en-vironment or ecosystems. Out of the demographic research in bio-logical, environmental, and social sciences has grown another focus of investigation that might become a science in its own right, called human ecology—referred to by Shepard and McKinely as the subversive science,[2] because the modern problems it seeks to deal with require totally new assessments and definitions regard-ing the questions, "What is man?" "What should he be doing?" and "What must he believe?" in order to increase the probability of survival. This also implies the question, "What ought man to quit doing?"

It is from the information provided by demographic statistical

[2] Paul Shepard, and Daniel McKinely, eds., *The Subversive Science* (Boston: Houghton Mifflin, 1969).

research (nose-counting, if you will) that an awareness is created regarding the social and ecological crises of modern man. It is in the inter-population differences in rates of employment, rates of disease, rates of infant mortality, rates of crime and legal adjudication, as examples, that the consequences of racial-ethnic or economic discrimination are most dramatically observable.

It is in the differential rates of urban vs. rural statistics of mental, physical, and social pathology that the unanticipated consequences of industrialization and urbanism become apparent and modern man's problems are defined.

Global Population Growth   Here is just one example of how statistical summarized information can create awareness of a problem. The growth and increased density of human populations is one indicator of change in man's ecosystem. We have just recently fully begun to realize the consequences of this change. Edward S. Deevy has provided the following information on this problem.[3]

Number of years ago	Density per sq. kilometer	Population in millions
1,000,000	0.004	0.13
300,000	0.012	1.00
25,000	0.040	3.34
10,000	0.040	5.32
6,000	1.000	86.50
2,000	1.000	133.00
310	3.700	545.00
210	4.900	728.00
160	6.200	906.00
60	11.000	1,610.00
10	16.400	2,400.00
A.D. 2,000	46.000	6,270.00

After remaining relatively steady for the major portion of man's history, the global population increased by 25 per cent between

---

[3] Edward S. Deevy, "The Human Population," in *The Subversive Science,* eds. Paul Shepard, and Daniel McKinely (Boston: Houghton Mifflin, 1969), p. 44. The article appeared in *Scientific American* in September, 1960. Copyright © 1960 by Scientific American, Inc. All rights reserved.

10,000 and 2,000 years ago, primarily because of food production capability and the settling of populations in stable living areas. However, in the 2,000 years since, the growth rate has been phenomenal and prognosis is a rate unheard of in man's history. Technology has greatly improved food production levels, medicine has reduced infant mortality and the effects of aging. Longevity is increasing to a point where most members of the species live to sexual maturity and reproduce themselves. The present crisis of overpopulation is most evident and man's knowledge has to be applied to the limitations of population if, in fact, he is to survive with a modicum of security. Present rates of increase are generally about 2.0 per cent per year. As Samuel Brody notes, if Adam and Eve had set up housekeeping 5,300 years ago and the rate of increase had been only 1.0 per cent per year for 5,300 years, and the average weight of any member of the earth's population was 100 pounds, the present population would equal the entire weight of the planet earth.[4] Therefore, one can readily see that the present rate of 2.0 per cent cannot go on indefinitely, especially when one considers 2.0 per cent of roughly three billion for this year alone.

Similarly, clues to the probable ecological bases for certain physical and mental illnesses can be found by statistical demographic analysis. Pinpointing high rates of a given pathology to specific geographic areas or among certain income levels may mean an important breakthrough in the analysis of the problem and such information in many cases has been available since the decade of the thirties. When a certain kind of pathology is seen to be associated with certain levels of population density or certain other demographic characteristics of that area, we may find that other kinds of things are similarly associated. Such an observation may then lead to a more specific study which results in the observance of a causal link between the pathology and one or more of the other associated variables of population density.

[4] Samuel Brody, "Facts, Foibles, and Fallacies on Feeding the World Population," in *The Subversive Science*, eds. Paul Shepard, and Daniel McKinely (Boston: Houghton Mifflin, 1969), p. 59.

Renewed Emphasis on the Sociology of Education and Socialization Because the decade of the sixties has been marked by a period of activism on college and university campuses (not to mention many high schools) directed at reform in society at large, as well as reform in educational processes, a renewed interest in the sociology of education has been sparked.

Demands for student involvement in the ongoing policy and decision-making activities of the university, demands for education that will be relevant preparation for living in the modern world, demands for application of scholarship, science, and technology to the solution of modern crises, demands for the realization of the American dream of equality and liberty in the pursuit of the good life, and demands for an open society and individual security from repressive political-economic systems have created a situation that engenders a reassessment, a reevaluation and, in all probability, a redesigning of the educational institutions of western society which serve as the recruitment and socializing agencies of the basic systems of the modern social system.

And, as mentioned earlier, the educational agency becomes the focal system interface at this point. As it does, many questions arise which require research and analysis of an elaborate nature for their answer. For example, are the students alienated because of the way we teach them, because of what we teach them, or because of what we do not teach them in our educational centers? What, after all, is teaching? How is it done? What is learning? How does one learn? Are we simply performing a traditional ritual or are we creating something for something? Do we know what we are supposed to be doing or want to be doing? Do we know why? Do we know what the consequences are? Are we afraid to ask? Are we to be the tools of an existing economic or political enterprise or are our concerns larger than these temporal and culture-specific and ever-changing priorities and interests? In short, what are the goals of the teaching and socializing of the young recruits to the social system and what are the most effective means (short-run and long-run) for achieving these goals? Are there any goals that are shared by all of the basic enterprises of society alike? And, if they could be found, how do they equate with the multifarious individual goals of all of society's members? Might we be better off trying to live with the reality of continued unrest and value conflict?

Perhaps the goal of education is to teach the appreciation and tolerance of difference. Hopefully, this would help society's members to become accustomed to an environment of change and ambiguity.

At any rate, the above is a fairly inclusive inventory of the questions which spark the present analytical concern in modern sociology regarding this emphasis. This book approaches answers only by implication, inasmuch as the lifework of at least another generation will be required before we will begin to have the answers to these questions.

The sociology of education has been a developing specialty in sociology for some time; however, most sociology of education courses have been geared to sociology for educators and, with a few notable exceptions, most research in this area has dealt with the application of sociological principles toward a variety of social problems related indirectly to education. With the renewed concern of the past decade, the direction of sociological research will be directed toward education as a social problem itself.

The notable exceptions of good research and analysis include studies directed toward career choice factors, research in the sociology of professions, and research in large-scale organizations as utilized by the administrative structures of educational units.

As sociologists attempt to answer the questions germane to the educational process, there will be a renewed involvement with psychology and theory and research which deal with the areas of human motivation, learning, and personality development.

As the information accumulates and as decisions are made to implement this knowledge for the ultimate design for effective education, a revolutionary structure will emerge—revolutionary in that educational processes will be brought into the twentieth century.

Steps are already being taken to implement a solution to the problem at the university level. Interestingly enough, the promoters of such schemes are on the margins or entirely outside of the traditional boundaries of the professorial profession. These promoters try to establish what are usually called free universities.

These free universities demonstrate varying kinds of success and follow a variety of patterns, but there are some common properties which have been provided by Ralph Keyes in a recent account of these activities. Generally, the emphasis is on:

1. Creating a new learning environment—escape from the large lecture class.
2. Focusing learning on more relevant, interesting, and integrated subjects—at least more contemporary applications.
3. Improved student-faculty relations—removing social distance from the classroom.
4. Broadening the pool of teachers—a more inclusive definition of what a teacher is.
5. Broadening the pool of students—a more inclusive definition of who can benefit from contact with the university.
6. Developing new subjects and teaching methods—"Kids are learning because they want to, not because they have to."[5]

If anything, the free universities and experimental colleges have pointed out to faculties in a most dramatic way that while most other modes of human cooperative activity have established twentieth century designs of structure and process, education is still largely utilizing nineteenth century models. Education is one of the few processes of modern society that only minimally utilizes the technological advances and the advances in knowledge about human behavior that have produced the modern phenomena. So much so that the young men and women (older ones, too) who have a real desire to teach the young find it almost impossible to do so within the existing educational structures. One has a distinct suspicion that they are training youth for professions that are all but obsolete.

Possible Directions of New Conceptual Approaches   In recent years individuals in the scholarly community have written innovative works which represent the rough outlines of new approaches to the conceptualization of human behavior and action. In fact,

---

[5] Ralph Keyes, "The Free Universities," in *The American Experience,* eds. Harold Jaffe, and John Tytell (New York: Harper and Row, 1970), pp. 177–189.

from some of these comes the explicit statement that they are indeed roughing in the broad outlines of new sciences. As yet, these works and their propagators have not been seriously accepted by the scholarly community in the mainstream of scientific interaction. However, they do have a fairly widespread readership and the language of their science is heard with increasing frequency. In time they will gain more attention from serious students of biology, anthropology, sociology, psychology, and the science of mass communication. It is the author's belief that the topics and approaches they use will become incorporated into the sub-specialties of the sociological enterprise within the next decade if student interest is any indicator of this probability.

Whether these approaches will become bona fide disciplines or not, only time will tell. However, the novel way in which the author conceptualizes the facets and determinants of individual and group behavior may very well produce some important breakthroughs in social research and aid in the solution of some present conceptual quagmires that traditional approaches have been unable to handle effectively. What follows is a brief resume of these two initial attempts at establishing a new conceptual framework.

Proxemics: Hall's *Hidden Dimension*—**Human Behavior in Physical Space**   Proxemics is the science which analyzes behavior, human and animal, as it relates to physical space and personal territory. As Hall describes it, the concern revolves around many kinds of descriptive accounts of space perception from culture to culture and from situation to situation. The concern is also with the effect of physical environment on mood, the effect of crowding on mood and behavior, the effect of variable distance between organisms and their behavior, differing definitions of space, territory, and behavior, and the various ways in which distance is used in communications between organisms.[6] What this all points to is a strong argument for the idea that the effects of crowding may have deleterious results in an overpopulated world long before the effects of limited foodstuffs are fully felt. It reinforces the cliché that man surely does not live by bread alone.

[6] Edward T. Hall, *The Hidden Dimension* (Garden City, N. Y.: Doubleday, Anchor, 1969), pp. 1–6.

Some of Hall's most interesting observations stem from the extrapolation of the ideas of such writers in ethology (the science of animal behavior) as Lorenz, Hediger, and Calhoun. These scientists are concerned with the effects of territoriality and space on animal populations, and Hall attempts to apply their findings to human populations. He advises the reader to keep in mind the great differences between animal and human behavior, but also advises that there may be more similarities in this regard than we presently appreciate. For example, deer flee when a human or another animal enters within the critical radius of their "flight distance." Will humans also exhibit stress or flight characteristics when their territorial bubble is entered by another organism? When the circumstances of situation and cultural training affecting human perception of critical distances (as defined by the particular context and the characteristics of the individuals concerned) are taken into account, it appears that this may be the case.

As regard these distinctions of social space or social definitions of distance, Hall has elaborated what appear to be universal human requirements dictated by the particular type of encounter between the individual and those who come into his territory (although these are slightly modified from culture to culture). His observations, made in several kinds of situations, suggest the following category of distances and the specific function of each. Hall indicates that the distances are predicated on sensory receptions of audio, visual, thermal, tactile, and olfactory stimuli (hearing, seeing, heat sensing, touch, and smell). He indicates four distance categories, each having two sub-categories:[7]

1. Intimate distance, 0–18 inches
     close phase, 0–6 inches
     far phase, 6–18 inches
2. Personal distance, 1.5–4 feet
     close phase, 1.5–2.5 feet
     far phase, 2.5–4 feet
3. Social distance, 4–12 feet
     close phase, 4–7 feet
     far phase, 7–12 feet

[7] *Ibid.*, pp. 110–119.

4. Public distance, 12–25 feet
close phase, 12–25 feet
far phase, 25 feet plus

Hall's general hypothesis concerning the function of these distance categories is this:

The specific distance chosen depends on the transaction, the relationship of the interacting individuals, how they feel, and what they are doing.[8]

Surely, there is nothing novel about this general hypothesis. The innovative character of Professor Hall's work is in specifying the factors which are implied in the hypothesis. This specification fosters an increased awareness regarding certain determinants of human behavior which have been neglected previously. In short, the specification of distance, kinds of transactions, kinds of relationships, types of individuals, categories of mood and human actions, and the possible relationships between these factors are of great importance to the continued investigation of human behavior.

Especially interesting is the investigation of the additional factor of sense stimulation as a communication mode related to distance. Too often our investigation of human interaction and intercommunication has focused mainly on verbal exchange or gestures. However, Hall suggests myriad subtle communications consciously received and sent and unconsciously received and sent which utilize the whole range of human senses. Beyond the senses of audio reception and visual reception are the highly sensitive receptions of surrounding stimuli which have been taken for granted without assessing their importance on human mood and interhuman communication. These are:

1. Thermal sensing—the reception of heat stimuli by the organism effects behavior change. How is the sensing of another's body heat defined by the individual in the context of the culture?

2. Tactile sensing—the reception of touch stimuli is of importance also. In what situations (social and cultural) can one

---

[8] *Ibid.,* p. 120.

be touched or touch another? What does touch communi-
cate? When is it acceptable and when is it taboo?

3. Olfactory stimuli—nasal reception of personal odors and
external environmental odors affects responses to other humans and to situations.

Continuing research in this area would then be in the direction
which would allow for the establishment of more exact knowledge
about the relationships between distance, excitation of senses
under different distance situations, and resulting kinds of anxiety
or nonanxiety responses. The consequences of such information
could be its utilization in the planning and construction of living
and working space that affords the maximum of social and psychological well-being for the human animal. Conversely, this could
also bring to a minimum the factors which contribute to the various
social and psychological pathologies of the crowded modern
urban man.

Eiconics: Boulding's *Images*—**The Effect of Imagery on Human
Behavior and Action**   Kenneth Boulding's *The Image*[9] was first
published in 1956, but it has been only in the last few years that it
has attracted attention in sociological circles. The book presents
an intriguing discussion concerned with the broad outlines of possibly another new science, which its author refers to as "Eiconics"
—the science of imagery, or what Walter Lippman once referred
to as "pictures in our heads."

In describing this new conceptual approach, Boulding does not
claim that he is the first to view human activity as being the result
of the image of the world held by the acting individual. From Plato
to Mannheim to Lippman, philosophers have pondered this relationship. Likewise in the realms of social psychology, anthropology, political science, and the science of communications, the
variable imagery of individuals and collectives has been of concern for research. Linguistics, symbolics, semantics, and syntac-
tics are areas of philosophical specialization which investigate
verbal and symbolic behavior. In recent intellectual history, from
Sigmund Freud to Herbert Mead to Norbert Wiener, the concern

[9] Kenneth Boulding, *The Image* (Ann Arbor: University of Michigan Press, 1956).

for imagery is of great importance. However, it is Boulding's intention that these various interdisciplinary activities be brought together, systematized, and organized into a unitary discipline. That is essentially what his book is an attempt to do—to rough in the bold outlines of a general theory of mental imagery, the communication of imagery from person to person and from generation to generation, and the effects of this shared imagery upon the collective human enterprise.

Moreover, it is an attempt to synthesize in a single text the general knowledge already accumulated regarding this phenomenon. In so doing, Boulding presents an elaboration of imagery as it relates to social organization, the biological organism, human behavior, economics, politics, history, and subcultures. In this context the sciences of human behavior become objects of analysis themselves, for the claim is that science itself is a shared image of the world.

Consistent with the thought that the ideas of man have a creative force, a theme quite prevalent in the works of Hegel, Kant, Weber, and Mannheim, Boulding notes how mankind's social organizations are modeled after images derived as analogues from biological or mechanical processes observable to man. Society is described in terms of its similarities to an organism, for example, or to a clock, and over time the metaphor becomes a definitional fact.

> Man's image is characterized by a capacity for internal growth and development quite independent from messages received from outside.[10]

He goes on to note that as we have made a metaphorical transference from physical process to ideas of social organization, we, in turn, design new modifications along the lines of mechanical design. The implication is that the control systems of modern organization, the administrative functionaries of society, have been given roles to perform based on the thermostats in mechanical systems. The question then arises, have we observed the realities

---

[10] *Ibid.,* p. 26.

of human organization or have we created an image that we now impose on reality?

Boulding sees this process as a two-way street. Images make society and society remakes images. He sees the bond which holds society together as the shared public image of its members. Therefore, the basic educational concern of a society is with the protection and transmission of its public imagery as a transcript handed from generation to generation. In primitive societies this is accomplished by verbal rituals. In modern society it is accomplished more and more in the rather disassociated way of mass media—"Generations yet unborn will see the 'D Day' landing" on their television sets, but how is it to be understood out of its historical context. In giving that context, technological society must more and more relay its public image in school rather than in experience.

Education is a matter of harnessing biological drives in the interest of establishing a value system of society.[11]

But, notes Boulding, the process of image transference from generation to generation is even at its best disconnected and lacking in integration. Bits and pieces of the transcript are thrown on the minds of the learners by various disciplines with varying degrees of success. Likewise there exist many interdisciplinary conflicts over the nature of the image. The result is that "out of intellectual pride we may be building a tower of Babel."

Whatever the future is for Boulding's Eiconics, the problems he poses and the avenues he suggests must surely find some protagonists in the sociological enterprise as it continues to develop knowledge about humans and why they do the things they do.

So ends this prognosis for the new sociology. A sketch methodically incomplete has its saving grace. It is presumptuous enough to make a prognosis, vague as it is, without committing the ultimate transgression of being specific and elaborate. Any meteorologist would tell you that. But, it is quite safe to say that sociolo-

[11] *Ibid.,* p. 73.

gists will continue in the direction of building a synthetic and analytic science that will at some time afford answers and problem solutions. There are a few answers already and some of these have been made available in this book. The reader, unless he is one of my learned colleagues, will have to admit he knows something now that he didn't know before reading the book. It may not be much, but the author must believe that it is important. No single book can tell it all, nor can any single science or course of study. No book or its author can educate. He and it can only point out a direction for the self-education of the inquiring mind.

Selected Bibliography

Aron, Raymond. *German Sociology.* Glencoe, Ill.: The Free Press, 1964.

————. *Main Currents in Sociological Thought;* Vols. I and II. New York: Basic Books, Inc., Publishers, 1967.

————. *Progress and Disillusion.* New York: New American Library (Mentor), 1968.

Bales, Robert F. *Interaction Process Analysis.* Cambridge, Mass.: Addison-Wesley, 1950.

Barber, Bernard. *Science and the Social Order.* New York: Collier Books, 1962.

Becker, Howard S. *The Outsiders.* New York: The Free Press, 1963.

Bell, Daniel. *The End of Ideology.* Glencoe, Ill.: The Free Press, 1960.

Bendix, Reinhard, and Lipset, Seymour, eds. *Class, Status and Power.* Glencoe, Ill.: The Free Press, 1953.

Bennett, John W., and Tumin, Melvin. *Social Life.* New York: Alfred A. Knopf, 1948.

Berelson, Bernard, and Steiner, Gary A. *Human Behavior.* New York: Harcourt Brace Jovanovich, 1964.

Bergmann, Gustav. *Philosophy of Science.* Madison: University of Wisconsin Press, 1958.

Blau, Peter, and Scott, Richard. *Formal Organizations.* San Francisco: Chandler Press, 1962.

Boguslaw, Robert. *The New Utopians.* Englewood Cliffs, N. J.: Prentice-Hall, 1965.

Boulding, Kenneth. *The Image.* Ann Arbor: University of Michigan Press, 1956.

Bredemeier, Harry C., and Stephenson, Richard M. *The Analysis of Social Systems.* New York: Holt, Rinehart and Winston, 1962.

Butterfield, Herbert. *The Origins of Modern Science 1300–1800,* rev. ed. New York: Macmillan, 1959.

Chinoy, Ely. *Society: An Introduction to Sociology.* New York: Random, 1962.

Clinard, Marshall, and Quinney, Richard. *Criminal Behavior Systems.* New York: Holt, Rinehart and Winston, 1967.

Cloward, Richard, and Ohlin, Lloyd. *Delinquency and Opportunity.* Glencoe, Ill.: The Free Press, 1960.

Cohen, Albert. *Delinquent Boys: The Culture of the Gang.* Glencoe, Ill.: The Free Press, 1964.

Coser, Lewis, and Rosenberg, Bernard, eds. *Sociological Theory: A Book of Readings,* 3rd ed. New York: Macmillan, 1969.

Crombie, Alistair C. *Medieval and Early Modern Science,* Vols. I and II. Cambridge: Harvard University Press, 1961.

Dahl, Robert A. *Modern Political Analysis.* Englewood Cliffs, N. J.: Prentice-Hall, 1964.

Domhoff, William. *Who Rules America?* Englewood Cliffs, N. J.: Prentice-Hall, 1967.

Etzioni, Amitai. *The Active Society.* New York: The Free Press, 1968.

Ferkiss, Victor. *Technological Man.* New York: New American Library, 1969.

Freund, Julien. *The Sociology of Max Weber.* New York: Random (Pantheon), 1968.

Gerth, Hans, and Mills, C. Wright. *From Max Weber: Essays in Sociology.* New York: Oxford University Press, 1946.

Gouldner, Alvin, and Gouldner, Helen. *Modern Sociology.* New York: Harcourt Brace Jovanovich, 1963.

Hall, Edward T. *The Hidden Dimension.* Garden City, N. Y.: Doubleday (Anchor), 1969.

Heinemann, F. H. *Existentialism and the Modern Predicament.* New York: Harper and Row, 1958.

Jaffe, Harold, and Tytell, John, eds. *The American Experience.* New York: Harper and Row, 1970.

Klausner, Samuel. *The Study of Total Societies.* Garden City, N. Y.: Doubleday (Anchor), 1967.

Lazarsfeld, Paul, and Rosenberg, Morris, eds. *The Language of Social Research.* Glencoe, Ill.: The Free Press, 1955.

Lipset, Seymour Martin, and Bendix, Reinhard. *Social Mobility in Industrial Society.* Berkeley: University of California Press, 1960.

Mannheim, Karl. *Ideology and Utopia.* New York: Harcourt, Brace & Company, Inc., 1936.

Martindale, Don. *Institutions, Organizations and Mass Society.* New York: Houghton Mifflin, 1966.

Mayer, J. P. *Max Weber and German Politics,* 2nd ed. London: Faber and Faber, 1956.

Merton, Robert. *Social Theory and Social Structure,* 6th ed. Glencoe, Ill.: The Free Press, 1962.

Michels, Robert. *Political Parties.* Glencoe, Ill.: The Free Press, 1949.

Mills, C. Wright. *Images of Man.* New York: George Braziller, 1960.

————. *The Power Elite.* New York: Oxford University Press (Galaxy), 1959.

Monane, Joseph. *The Sociology of Human Systems.* New York: Appleton-Century-Crofts, 1967.

Niebuhr, Reinhold. *Moral Man and Immoral Society.* New York: Charles Scribner's, 1932.

Parsons, Talcott. *The Structure of Social Action.* New York: McGraw-Hill, 1937.

————, and Shils, Edward. *Toward a General Theory of Action.* New York: Harper (Torchbooks), 1965.

Pfuetze, Paul. *Self, Society and Existence.* New York: Harper and Row, 1961.

Rheinstein, Max, ed. and trans. *Max Weber on Law and Economy in Society.* New York: Simon and Schuster (Clarion), 1967.

Ross, E. A. *Social Control.* New York: Macmillan, 1928.

Roszak, Theodore. *The Making of a Counter Culture.* New York: Doubleday, 1969.

Shepard, Paul, and McKinely, Daniel, eds. *The Subversive Science.* Boston: Houghton Mifflin, 1969.

Shepherd, Clovis. *Small Groups: Some Sociological Perspectives.* San Francisco: Chandler Press, 1964.

Shibutani, Tamotsu. *Society and Personality.* Englewood Cliffs, N. J.: Prentice-Hall, 1961.

Simmel, Georg. *Conflict.* Trans. Kurt H. Wolff. Glencoe, Ill.: The Free Press, 1955.

Sjoberg, Gideon. *Ethics, Politics and Social Research.* Cambridge, Mass.: Schenkman Publishing, 1967.

Sorokin, Pitirim. *Contemporary Sociological Theories.* New York: Harper (Torchbooks), 1964.

_____. *The Crisis of Our Age.* New York: E. P. Dutton, 1941.

Spencer, Herbert. *The Study of Sociology.* New York: D. Appleton & Co., 1873.

Stein, Maurice, et al., eds. *Identity and Anxiety.* Glencoe, Ill.: The Free Press, 1963.

Storer, Norman. *The Social System of Science.* New York: Holt, Rinehart and Winston, 1966.

Sutherland, Edwin, and Cressey, Donald. *Principles of Criminology,* 6th ed. New York: Lippincott, 1960.

Taber, William, ed. *Man in Contemporary Society.* New York: Columbia University Press, 1962.

Thrasher, Frederic M. *The Gang.* Chicago: University of Chicago Press, 1927.

Timasheff, Nicholas. *Sociological Theory.* New York: Random, 1967.

Watson, James. *The Double Helix.* New York: Atheneum, 1968.

Weber, Max. *The Sociology of Religion.* Trans. Ephraim Fischoff. Boston: Beacon Press, 1963.

_____. *The Theory of Social and Economic Organization.* Trans. A. M. Henderson, and Talcott Parsons. New York: Oxford University Press, 1947.

Whyte, William F. *Street Corner Society.* Chicago: University of Chicago Press, 1943.

Yinger, Milton. *Religion, Society and the Individual.* New York: Macmillan, 1957.

Zeitlin, Irving. *Ideology and the Development of Sociological Theory.* Englewood Cliffs, N. J.: Prentice-Hall, 1968.

Index